S

Discovering and Mastering

Single Malt Scotch
WHISKY

NYC 2014

To kelly,
Great meeting you at whisky
Jubilee.
Hope you enjoy this book as
much as I enjoyed writing it.
See you at Koval.
Cheers!

Sébastien

Discovering & Mastering Single Malt Scotch WHISKY

Copyright © Sébastien Gavillet, 2012
E: admin@winevibe.com
W: www.whiskyvibe.com

Bære & Uvæ Publishing Company
T:+1-702-234-3602
E: admin@bupublishing.com
W: www.bupublishing.com

The moral right of the author has been asserted.

ISBN-13: 978-0-9887562-1-2
Library of Congress Control Number: 2013933419

First American Paperback Edition - February 2013

Cover Design by Yulia Andreyeva & Sébastien Gavillet
Book Design by Miroslav Suster & Sébastien Gavillet
Copywriter: Jinky Bagagnan
Editor: Joyous A. Seeman
Maps & illustrations by Yulia Andreyeva

Dedication:
To my wife, family and friends – for sharing my passion, for your abiding support, for your unstinting encouragement, and for the many glasses shared – this book is for you.
To Kiki, you remain and will always be in our hearts.

Acknowledgments go out to:
Master Mixologist Francesco Lafranconi, for sharing his expertise and letting me use his recipes.
Jinky, for all her work on this book.

Printed in the USA

TABLE OF CONTENTS

❀Introduction❀

W hat is whisky? Or is it supposed to be whiskey? Whisky, whiskey—does it matter? What is Single Malt Scotch? How is it made? What are pot stills? Does the type of still affect the taste of the spirit? Is the water source relevant? Islay, Highlands, Lowlands, Speyside, etc.—do production regions matter in Scotch the way appellations matter in wines?

This book answers all of these questions and more. In its pages, one will learn all the information needed to be knowledgeable about Scotch Whisky in general and Single Malt Scotch Whisky in particular.

There are already many fine publications on the subject of Single Malt Scotch. A lot of them are quite exemplary, too, packed with technical and factual information that is valuable to Single Malt Scotch Whisky connoisseurs. In light of this fact, one might wonder why I saw the need to write this book at all. *Discovering and Mastering Single Malt Scotch Whisky* is NOT a replacement for the many superb publications already in print. Rather, it is meant to be a companion—a supplement, if you will—to such publications.

This book's value lies not only in the wealth of information it provides, but also in its unique organization and treatment of the subject matter, providing as much insight as needed without overloading casual readers with information they may not need or might not be ready to assimilate.

In this book, one will find simple, uncomplicated answers to the most common Single Malt

Scotch Whisky questions. Someone new to the world of Single Malt Scotch Whisky can use it as a starting point on their journey of Single Malt Scotch discovery, something they can read to learn more about the spirit, and also to gain a deeper knowledge about the topic. Someone with a more advanced knowledge, on the other hand, can use it as a general reference—something to whip out at a moment's notice to find answers to random questions that suddenly crop up in general conversations.

This book is a straightforward guide to the world of Single Malt Scotch—no more, no less. It does not aim to provide the reader with encyclopedic knowledge on the subject. What it does, instead, is give the reader a greater understanding of Single Malt Scotch for the purpose of increasing his appreciation of and respect for the spirit. Just like the way a map helps tourists navigate, so they can better enjoy unfamiliar territory, *Discovering and Mastering Single Malt Scotch Whisky* teaches whisky lovers the things they need to know to better enjoy every sip of their Single Malt Scotch Whisky.

Since this book has been written specifically to increase one's enjoyment of Single Malt Scotch, I made sure to include an extensive discussion on whisky aromas and flavors, whisky-tasting methods, and whisky etiquette. This book will teach skills that can be immediately applied and practiced. This is an important feature of this book because tasting and evaluating whisky can be a real challenge. You might have noticed how reviews of Single Malt Scotch Whiskies can vary significantly.

The differences are superficial rather than fundamental, caused in my opinion by the lack of a universal method of describing whisky. In fact, someone with a deep understanding of Single Malt Scotch should easily be able to see the common thread running through apparently dissimilar reviews.

Unfortunately, someone new to the world of Single Malt Scotch will not find it easy to do the same. It is for this reason that this book expounds on the method of tasting, enjoying, and then reviewing Single Malt Scotch Whisky. This way, I hope that I can help my readers along the road of Single Malt Scotch *Discovery* until they reach Single Malt Scotch *Mastery*.

So read on, fellow lover of Single Malt Scotch Whisky. I hope you enjoy this book as much as I enjoyed writing it. I hope it will answer the many questions you have about this very special spirit that the Scots have so aptly named *"uisge beatha"*—the water of life.

Sébastien Gavillet

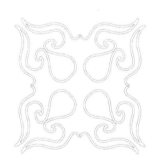

•Chapter 1•

The Basics

Single Malt Scotch Whisky is a type of Scotch Whisky. To understand it fully, you should first learn more about whisky and Scotch Whisky.

In this chapter, you will learn the basic facts that any lover of Single Malt Scotch Whisky knows by heart. This chapter will teach you the difference between whisky and whiskey, the characteristics of Scotch Whisky, and that which sets Single Malt Scotch Whisky apart from other types of Scotch Whisky.

SHOULD IT BE WHISKY OR WHISKEY?

The terms whisky and whiskey refer to the same type of distilled spirit. Is there a difference between the two? Apart from their

spelling – no. Whisky and whiskey both come from "uisge" of the Gaelic word "uisge beatha" which, literally translated, means "water of life."

However, this difference in spelling is far from inconsequential, so don't let it trip you up. If you are referring to whisky from Scotland (i.e., Scotch), use whisky. Whisky is also the preferred term if the distiller is from Canada, Germany, Finland, Wales, Australia, Japan, India, and most other countries.

Copper wash still used for making whisky

Whiskey, on the other hand, should be used when referring to whiskey from Ireland. This is also the preferred spelling when referring to whiskey from the United States.

Rule of thumb: When reviewing or writing about a particular whisk(e)y, respect the distiller's preference. If the label on the bottle says "whisky," use "whisky." If the label says "whiskey," use "whiskey."

WHAT IS WHISKY OR WHISKEY?

Whisky or whiskey is an alcoholic beverage produced by fermenting and then distilling mashed grain.

There are many types of whisk(e)y.

Some whiskies/whiskeys are made from a single type of grain, while others are made from a mixture of grains. Some distilleries use only malted grains, while others use a mixture of malted and unmalted grains.

Some whiskies/whiskeys are produced using pot stills, others are not (for instance, some are produced using Coffey stills). Some are a product of a single distillery, while some are a mixture of whiskies/whiskeys distilled by two or more distilleries.

WHAT IS SCOTCH WHISKY?

Scotch Whisky (also known simply as Scotch) is whisky from

Scotland that meets the production guidelines set forth in the Scotch Whisky Regulations.

Characteristics of Scotch Whisky

Below, you will find a discussion on the defining characteristics of Scotch Whisky. Unless otherwise specified, these characteristics apply to all types of Scotch Whisky, including Single Malt Scotch Whisky.

Produced using malted barley

Malted barley (also known simply as malt) is the basic ingredient of Scotch Whiskies. While it is the only type of grain or cereal used in making Single Malt Scotch Whisky, whole grains of other cereals may be added to malted barley if making Grain Scotch Whisky.

Note: Distilleries can make their own malt, or they can obtain malted barley from independent malt houses or companies that specialize in making malt.

Made in a distillery in Scotland

The malted barley (plus supplementary grains if the distillery is using any) should be mashed and fermented in the same distillery that is distilling the Scotch Whisky.

Grains prepared for fermentation using endogenous enzyme systems

Scotch Whisky distillers may not use grains that have been prepared for fermentation through the use or addition of artificial enzymes.

Prior to fermentation, the barley's starch content must be converted to sugar, and certain enzymes must act on the grains for this conversion to occur. For the purposes of making Scotch Whisky, it is crucial that the grains be allowed to produce these enzymes endogenously (note that endogenous means "synthesized from within"). The production of these endogenous enzymes is the purpose of malting.

Fermented only with the addition of yeast

After the grains have been adequately prepared for fermentation, only yeast may be added to initiate fermentation.

Alcoholic strength by volume must fall within set limits

Scotch Whisky has an alcoholic strength by volume of at least 40% but less than 94.8%. If the alcoholic strength by volume is 94.8% or greater, Scotch loses the distinct color, aroma, and taste derived from its raw materials and its unique production methods.

Distinct color, aroma, and taste

Whiskies produced in Scotland distilleries all undergo evaluation and testing to ensure that they have been able to retain the distinct color, aroma, and taste derived from the raw materials that were used as well as the Scotch Whisky production and maturation methods that were followed.

Matured or aged in oak casks

All Scotch Whiskies undergo a standard maturation process. Scotch is matured for at least three years in oak casks, the capacity of which must not exceed 700 liters or 184.92 U.S. gallons.

Matured or aged in Scotland

Scotch Whisky must be aged in Scotland, specifically in an excise warehouse or some other permitted facility within Scotland. Whisky produced by a distillery in Scotland, when matured outside Scotland, automatically loses its right to the Scotch Whisky designation.

Restrictions on additional substances

Only water and/or plain caramel coloring may be added to Scotch Whisky.

Moved out of Scotland in an approved container

Scotch Whisky, after sufficient maturation in an oak cask at an approved facility in Scotland, cannot be exported in oak or wooden casks. Scotch Whisky can be exported only after bottling or, if sold in bulk, it must be transported in a non-wooden container (say, containers made of plastic or steel).

On November 23, 2012, the regulations concerning the export of

Single Malt Scotch Whisky became even stricter. Single Malt Scotch Whisky may no longer be exported in bulk but must now be bottled in Scotland (with the bottle labeled for retail sale) before export.

Categories of Scotch Whisky

Scotch Whisky has five categories:

- **Single Malt Scotch Whisky**
- **Single Grain Scotch Whisky**
- **Blended Malt Scotch Whisky**
- **Blended Grain Scotch Whisky**
- **Blended Scotch Whisky**

However, there are only two basic types of Scotch Whisky: Single Malt Scotch and Single Grain Scotch. It is from these two basic types that the three remaining categories are derived.

Single Malt Scotch Whisky

For a detailed discussion of Single Malt Scotch, see "What is Single Malt Scotch Whisky?" in the next section.

Single Grain Scotch Whisky

Single Grain Scotch Whisky is distilled in a single distillery (thus the word "Single" in its name). It is made with water, malted barley, and other types of whole grains. Examples of whole grains that may be added to malted barley when making Single Grain Scotch are unmalted barley, malted wheat, unmalted wheat, malted corn, and unmalted corn.

Blended Malt Scotch Whisky

Blended Malt Scotch Whisky is simply a blend of two or more

Single Malt Scotch Whiskies. The Single Malt Scotch Whiskies used in the blend must have been distilled in two or more distilleries in Scotland.

Blended Grain Scotch Whisky

Blended Grain Scotch Whisky refers to a mixture of two or more Single Grain Scotch Whiskies. The Single Grain Scotch Whiskies used in the blend must have been distilled in two or more distilleries in Scotland.

Blended Scotch Whisky

Blended Scotch Whisky is a mixture of a Single Malt Scotch Whisky (or two or more Single Malt Scotch Whiskies) AND a Single Grain Scotch Whisky (or two or more Single Grain Scotch Whiskies). To put it simply, it is a blend of Single Malt Scotch Whisky/Whiskies AND Single Grain Scotch Whisky/Whiskies.

WHAT IS SINGLE MALT SCOTCH WHISKY?

Single Malt Scotch Whisky refers to a distinct Scotch Whisky category. Among all the types of Scotch Whisky, Single Malt Scotch has the strongest flavor and the most character, and, for this reason, it has a great following worldwide. Single Malt Scotch Whiskies also rank among the most expensive whiskies in the world.

Characteristics of Single Malt Scotch

Aside from conforming to the minimum standards of production laid out for Scotch Whisky by the Scotch Whisky Regulations, Single Malt Scotch Whisky has several special characteristics.

Malted barley as the only grain ingredient

Single malt is distilled from water and malted barley in one or more batches. No other cereal may be used or added.

Produced by a single distillery

The word "Single" in Single Malt Scotch Whisky refers to the fact that anything being sold or marketed as Single Malt Scotch Whisky must have been distilled by a single distillery.

Distilled using a pot still

A pot still is a type of distillation equipment. Pot still distillation is a definite requirement when making Single Malt Scotch Whisky.

Bottled in Scotland

Since November 23, 2012, all Single Malt Scotch Whiskies must be bottled in Scotland, and the bottle must be labeled for retail sale.

•Chapter II•

The History of Single Malt Scotch Whisky

How did Single Malt Scotch Whisky come to be? The answer to this question may not matter much to most people, but it sure does to lovers of Single Malt Scotch.

This chapter discusses the history of Single Malt Scotch Whisky and the laws that have influenced its growth and development through the years. Also included are historical references to whisky in Scotland.

ORIGIN OF SCOTCH WHISKY

Before there was Scotch Whisky, there was *uisge beatha*.

Uisge beatha is the forerunner of Scotch Whisky. In fact, the word *whisky* is derived from the term *uisge* in *uisge beatha*, which is Scottish Gaelic for water of life.

In historical records, Scotch Whisky was also commonly referred to as *aqua vitae*, which is simply Latin for water of life.

It is not clear when *uisge beatha* became *whisky*. It is not even clear when the Scots started distilling this alcoholic spirit. Some say whisky (or *uisge beatha* or *aqua vitae*) existed in Scotland before the fifteenth century; others are convinced that the lack of references to whisky in pre-fifteenth-century Scottish historical records prove otherwise.

So, when exactly was Scotch Whisky invented? The earliest recorded (known) reference to the production of Scotch Whisky can be found in the records of the Exchequer (the department in charge of overseeing the Royal Household's finances) for 1494. Other references to aqua vitae appeared recurrently in the Lord High Treasurer's Accounts as well as in the Exchequer Rolls during the reign of King James IV.

The 1494 Exchequer Rolls entry read:

"Eight bolls of malt to Friar John Cor wherewith to make aqua vitae."

This record proves that Scotch Whisky existed in the fifteenth century. However, this does not necessarily mean that Scotch Whisky was invented in the late fifteenth century. According to the Scotch Whisky Association, this quantity of malt is enough to make around fifteen-hundred bottles of whisky, thereby indicating that whisky distillation was "already well-established" at that time.[1] Indeed, it is possible that the Scots began distilling Scotch Whisky earlier than the late fifteenth century.

HISTORY OF SCOTCH WHISKY

While we cannot be sure of when malt whisky distillation began in Scotland, it is clear that distillation is not a Scottish invention. The art of distillation was developed elsewhere (the history of distillation is discussed in greater detail in the next chapter if you are interested). Somehow, knowledge about distillation techniques reached Scotland (supposedly through Irish monks). The Scots, ingenious people that they are, then applied these techniques to come up with—yup, you guessed it—Scotch Whisky (i.e., *uisge beatha* or aqua vitae as they called it in those days).

The Monks' and Barber-Surgeons' Monopoly

The Exchequer Rolls entry mentioned earlier substantiates the fact that early Single Malt Scotch was mainly (albeit perhaps not exclusively) distilled inside monasteries. The commonly held belief that whisky has medicinal qualities probably spurred on the monks' continued study and development of whisky distillation.

Outside Scottish monasteries, Scotch Whisky distillation was the province of barber-surgeons. This was borne out by Treasury records in 1498 as well as the charter of the Barber-Surgeons Guild of Edinburgh (1505).

However, the monks' and barber-surgeons' monopoly over Scotch Whisky distillation was soon to end.

The Spread of Scotch Whisky Distillation

In the late sixteenth century, whisky distillation became relatively widespread in Scotland's farming communities.[2] Scotch Whisky distillation techniques also grew considerably more advanced during the sixteenth and seventeenth centuries.[3] So, what happened to make Scotch Whisky distillation a relatively "common" craft?

The displacement of monks in the late sixteenth century is the most likely explanation. In 1587, the Scottish Parliament passed an Act called the Annexation of the Temporalities of Benefices to the Crown. This Act led to the dissolution of monasteries, priories, abbeys, and other such religious sanctuaries in Scotland. Persons of the clergy, forced out of their secure berths, suddenly had to make a living outside monastic walls.

It is possible that displaced monks earned money by applying the skills they had developed and mastered inside the monasteries. Those who were skilled in the craft of medicine probably treated patients. Those who were skilled in the craft of carpentry probably hired themselves out to build houses and furniture.

It is reasonable to expect that those who were skilled in Scotch Whisky distillation made and sold Scotch Whisky. They might even have taken in apprentices, whom they could have taught what they knew about Scotch Whisky distillation.

In any case, around the time the monks were forced out of the monasteries, knowledge of Scotch Whisky distillation spread across Scotland; Scotch Whisky distillation grew more advanced, and farmers and ordinary folks learned and mastered the art of making Scotch Whisky.

The Evolution of Scotch Whisky

Even when Scotch Whisky distillation was mainly contained within monasteries, Scotch Whisky was already an integral part of the Scots' lives. It was mainly popular for its perceived medicinal qualities. Even so, it was more than just a cure for ailments; whisky was also a drink that the Scots imbibed socially.

The spread of whisky distillation knowledge that (we assume) came with the displacement of Scottish monks probably propelled Scotch Whisky to new heights. It meant a greater supply of and a greater access to Scotch Whisky; it also meant more advanced whisky distillation techniques. In fact, whisky became so popular in Scotland that the Scottish Parliament actually had to place a temporary ban on whisky distillation in 1579 to ensure that the expected short-term malt shortage would not be aggravated by distillers who would have used enormous quantities of malt to make whisky.

Taxes and More Taxes

The obvious popularity of Scotch Whisky would not have escaped the notice of the authorities—and this was made clear in 1644. When money was needed to sustain and maintain the army, the Parliament of Scotland levied excise duties on certain commodities—and one of the excisable commodities named in this Act of Parliament is whisky.

The 1644 Excise on aqua vitae opened a door that could never be again closed. After 1644, the excise on whisky varied in nature and severity, but it never really went away and, through the years, it stayed on a generally upward course (until 1707). Then in 1661, duties no longer applied only to whisky but also to malt. This annexed excise on malt was dissolved in 1695 – but this also meant that additional excise du-

ties on whisky had to be levied to ensure that the Crown's income would not suffer unduly.

The increasing and often multiple taxes on whisky put a great burden on the whisky distillers. The Scottish Parliament would sometimes set whisky prices in an effort to ensure that the whisky distillers would be assured of profits after taxes.

The greatest challenge to the industry of Scotch Whisky distillation, however, was yet to come in the form of the 1707 Act of Union, the "Act Ratifying and Approving the Treaty of Union of the Two Kingdoms of Scotland and England." This Act of Union provides that the Kingdoms of Scotland and England shall be merged into one Kingdom—the United Kingdom of Great Britain—effective May 1st.

The 1707 Act of Union assigned the job of excise collection on liquor to a central Boards of Excise. This meant excise payments were collected according to the schedule of the United Kingdom's excise collection and no longer according to the distillers' convenience. The English excise collectors, moreover, were stricter than the former (Scottish) excise collectors; distillers had to pay up or face grave consequences.

Dissatisfaction with the Union was felt even more keenly by the distillers when, in 1713, the

Parliament of Great Britain extended the malt tax that existed in England to Scotland. The Scottish distillers felt even more persecuted when, in 1725, the tax on malt was increased. Violent protests leading to the damage of property and loss of lives followed. After 1725, the malt tax was increased several more times.

The high taxes meant higher operating costs and very marginal profits. Unable (and unwilling) to pay the taxes, whisky distillers started hiding their distillation activities from the gaugers or the excisemen—and so began the moonshine phase of whisky distillation.

Moonshine Phase

The Scots distillers responded to the higher taxes by hiding their caches of malt whisky. They started making whisky at night so that the darkness would disguise the black smoke from their pot stills. It was at this time that Scotch Whisky gained the nickname Scottish Moonshine, a reference to the fact that the Scots distilled their whisky only at night.

The Scots distillers made their whisky illegally, but by all accounts, they appeared to have the support of their neighbors. They would post lookouts at various points in their villages, so they would be warned if and when excisemen came. This way, most of the unlicensed distillers evaded capture and continued to make malt whisky; they even smuggled their tax-free whisky to England.

Of course, there were licensed distillers at this time. However, the number of licensed distillers was incongruously disproportionate to Scotland's actual volume of whisky production. Incidentally, it was during the moonshine phase that whisky made from non-malted barley was introduced. Licensed distillers had to use non-malted barley in an effort to reduce their production costs.

Note: Non-malted or unmalted barley is barley that has not been malted; malting is the process that converts the grains' starch content to sugar. Since malted barley was heavily taxed and therefore expensive, distillers had to supplement or replace malted barley with unmalted barley when they distilled whisky. Whisky made from grains other than or in addition to malted barley is known as grain whisky; on the other hand, whisky made from malted barley is known as malt whisky.

During the Scottish Moonshine phase, the Government of Great Britain tried all measures to stop the illicit distillation and smuggling of whisky. Homemade whisky was taxed, other types of taxes were introduced, production restrictions were set up, and other measures were put in place – but moonshine distilling remained and flourished.

The Scottish Moonshine phase ended only when the government finally realized that they had lost more revenue than they had gained by heavily taxing whisky distillers. After all, they could not benefit from taxes they could not collect.

Thus, in 1823, the Excise Act was passed. Under this Act, distillers could distill whisky legally for a license fee of £10 payable annually. Computing tax dues was also greatly simplified with the introduction of a fixed rate per gallon of alcohol produced. Immediately after the Excise Act

of 1823 was instituted, the number of licensed distillers ballooned from a mere handful to more than a hundred.

Today, malt whisky production continues to thrive in Scotland. Single Malt Scotch is still one of the most popular types of Scotch Whisky; it is also one of the most popular types of malt whisky in the world.

Note: Malt whisky production is not exclusive to Scotland. Other countries produce their own malt whiskies and, as discussed in the earlier chapter, Scotland produces other whiskies aside from the single malt variety. However, only malt whiskies made and aged in Scotland and produced as per the Scotch Whisky Regulations can be called Single Malt *Scotch* Whisky.

RELEVANT LEGISLATION OF THE OLD SCOTTISH PARLIAMENT

In this section, you will find a list and a brief description of the Acts of the old Scottish Parliament that had or continue to have an effect on the Scotch Whisky industry.

Note: References to money, unless otherwise specified, are in Scottish currency. When used in the context of money, "*s*" stands for shilling and "*d*" stands for penny. Example: 8*s* 4*d* means 8 shillings and 4 pence. Additionally, 1 merk is equivalent to 13 shillings and 4 pence (i.e., 13*s* 4*d*).

Concerning Maltmakers (1552)[4]

This item stipulates that for a period of one year, makers of malt shall, for each boll of malt they produce, have 4*s* more than the selling price of a boll of barley. This piece of legislation was instituted for the sake of ensuring fair market prices for malt.

Concerning the Possession of Tallow, Victuals, and Meat Out of This Realm (1555)[5]

This is one of the pieces of legislation passed on the 20th of June by the Scottish Parliament of Mary I, Queen of Scots. It prohibits anyone—subjects of the Kingdom and strangers alike—from carrying victuals, tallow, or meat out of the realm. Travelers are also instructed to carry just enough provender for their trip, obviously with the intent of limiting the unintended flow of essential supplies out of Scotland and into other territories.

This law makes it clear, however, that it will always be lawful for residents of the burghs of Ayr,

Irvine, Glasgow, Dumbarton, or other places at the west seas to trade baked bread, brewed ale, and whisky for other merchandise. The exception to the export prohibition also naturally extends to the operators of the vessels used by these traders to transport their goods.

Papal Jurisdiction Act (1560)[6]

This Act of Parliament states that the Bishop of Rome, the Pope, no longer has any jurisdiction and authority in Scotland. Thus, the subjects of the Kingdom must not seek any title or rights from the Pope. Those who are found guilty of violating this law will be punished with proscription; they will also be banished from the realm and disqualified from holding public office.

This was a key piece of legislation, without which it would have been nearly impossible to enforce the abolition of the religious sanctuaries in Scotland in 1587—the event which most likely jumpstarted the spread of whisky distillation knowledge in Scotland.

Concerning the Making of Aquavitae (1579)[7]

This Act, legislated by the Scottish Parliament on 11th November 1579 in response to an expected short-term shortage of malt, made it illegal to distill aqua vitae from 1st December 1579 up to 1st October 1580. Under this law, violation of the whisky distillation ban meant confiscation of the illegally distilled whisky as well as breaking of the equipment owned and used by those involved in its production. The ban, however, did not apply to noblemen, who could still distill whisky using their own malt, within their own estate, for their and their friends' consumption.

Annexation of the Temporalities of Benefices to the Crown (1587)[8]

This Act of Parliament annexes to or appropriates for the Crown (with specific exceptions) all lands, mansions, towers, parks, woods, mills, towns, villages, tenants, the free service of said tenants, profits, and all other assets, commodities, and equipment that, on the day of the Act's legislation (i.e., 29th July 1587), belong to ecclesiastical or beneficed persons. Under this Act, the profits pertaining to the annexed properties (i.e., the profits of abbeys, priories, convents, cloisters, monasteries, and all other non-exempt religious sanctuaries) shall be levied starting on 11th November 1587.

This Act had an indirect influence over the development of whisky distillation techniques in seventeenth-century Scotland. The annexation of the lands and other properties belonging to the church meant the displacement of the monks and other members of the clergy. Forced to live outside the monasteries and various sanctuaries, these monks had to earn a living, and it was likely that at least some of them did so by distilling and then selling whisky. This is theorized to have been instrumental in the spread and advancement of Scotch Whisky distillation knowledge in Scotland.

Act Discharging the Importation of Strong Waters (1641)[9]

Dated 16th November 1641, this protectionist Act of Parliament prohibits the import of aqua vitae or strong waters to Scotland under the pain of escheat or the confiscation of the illegally imported spirit.

Excise (1644)[10]

This Act, dated 31st January 1644, was established to ensure that the Royal Government will have sufficient funds to support the Scottish army in England and Ireland. Under this Act, certain commodities are to be subject to the payment of excise. Aqua vitae is one of these commodities. Specifically, every pint of aqua vitae or strong waters sold within the country is to be levied a tax of 2s 8d.

Act and Commission Anent the Excise (1647)[11]

This Act, dated 10th March 1647, outlines the procedures for collecting taxes on commodities subject to excise, specifies the commodities subject to excise and their respective rates, stipulates how collected funds would be allocated, and names the excise commissioners.

According to this Act, excise on the

taxable commodities shall be levied *"over and above all customs and other duties due and payable for the same"* and shall last until 1st January 1648. The excise shall be levied starting on 12th March for wine. For all other commodities, the excise shall start taking effect on 20th March for South of River Tay and on 30th March for North of River Tay.

Act for Raising the Annuity of £40,000 Sterling Granted to His Majesty (1661)[12]

The Scottish Parliament, through this Act dated 29th March 1661, decides to fund a large part of the King's annual annuity of £480,000 (in Scots currency) by taxing malt, its end products and other alcoholic beverages. The levy applies to commodities traded or sold for profit—unless the burgh is short of its excise quota.

The following is a list of the applicable rates:

- 2 merks per boll of malt brewed
- 3s per pint of domestic whisky or strong waters (not made of malt)
- 6s per pint of imported whisky or strong waters
- 12s per barrel of imported beer

Act in Favour of the Town of Edinburgh (1662)[13]

This Act, dated 26th August 1662, gives and grants Edinburgh (effective on the 1st of September next) *"16d upon every pint of Spanish and Rhenish wines, aquavitae and other strong liquors"* (also 8d on every pint of French wine) sold within the territory it holds and controls.

Act Discharging the Importation of Strong Waters, etc (1663)[14]

Instituted by the Scottish Parliament on 17th July 1663, this Act makes importing aqua vitae (also mum beer and other beer for drinking except spruce beer) illegal in Scotland. The punishment for violating this law is escheat of the imported beer or spirit.

Note: Mum beer can refer to a strong German beer or to a type of beer brewed and fermented from cereals, beans, etc.[15] Spruce beer is spruce-flavored beer. The shoots, cones, twigs, and/or needles of the spruce tree are usually boiled in water to extract the spruce flavor, after which the extracted essence is combined and allowed to ferment with the rest of the ingredients to give the resulting beer a distinct spruce aroma and flavor.

Act for Continuation of the Excise (1681)[16]

Promulgated by the Parliament of King Charles II on 6th September 1681, this Act provides for a 5-year extension on the 1661 excise on domestic and imported commodities, *"particularly of the 2 merks Scots upon each boll of malt, brewed and sold within the kingdom, and 3s Scots upon each pint of aqua-vitae and strong waters, not made of malt brewed and sold within this kingdom."* This continuation, set to commence upon the termination of the existing excise, was instituted to ensure that the Kingdom's finances will remain stable in case of the death of the current Regent.

A Declaration and Offer of Duty by the Kingdom of Scotland, with an Annexation of the Excise to the Crown (1685)[17]

Dated 28th April 1685, this declaration permanently annexes to the Crown the excise duties established in the 1661 Act of Parliament, the effective period of which was extended by the 1681 Act for Continuation of the Excise. This ensures that, at the end of the 5-year excise levied on malt and its end products by the 1681 Act of Parliament, the Crown will still have ample means of support.

This Act's excises, which will be in effect from the next 1st of May, shall for six months follow the rates and procedures prescribed by the 1661 Act of Parliament. After this six-month transition period, the procedures and rates prescribed by the 1681 Act of Parliament shall be followed.

This 1685 Act is different from both the 1661 and the 1681 excise laws in one crucial way. Under this Act, the excise duties shall be levied not for a temporary period (as in the 1681 Act) nor for the life of the current Regent (as in the 1661 Act) but for "all time coming" (unless it is repealed, of course), thereby ensuring that the Crown—that is to say, the present monarch and his heirs and successors—will have a stable source of income.

Act for Additional Excise (1693)[18]

On 5th May 1693, the Scottish Parliament debated the additional excise to levy on aqua vitae. It was ultimately decided that the additional excise be set at 2s.

Act for the Additional and Annexed Excises (1695)[19]

Dated 16th July 1695, this Act levies additional excise on alcoholic beverages, including whisky (specifically 2s per pint of spirit not made of malt), that have been brewed to be sold within the Kingdom. This additional excise, to be levied for a 12-month period, shall commence on the 1st of September next.

This Act also dissolves the 2-merk excise on each boll of malt that has been annexed to the Crown in the 1685 Act of Parliament. To alleviate the loss of revenues that will result from this dissolution of the annexed excise, additional excises on ale, beer, and whisky or strong waters (again, as long as they have been brewed for sale) are annexed in its place. These annexed excises will commence on the same date, the next 1st of September and shall be in force in perpetuity (unless of course it is repealed by a future sovereign).

On whisky or strong waters not made of malt, the annexed excise that will be levied over and above the earlier mentioned un-annexed excise is 3s. Whisky and strong waters made of malt shall be levied an additional annexed excise duty of 6s.

Act for an Additional Excise (1696)[20]

Dated 25th September 1696, this Act provides for an increase in the annexed excises on alcoholic beverages sold within the Kingdom of Scotland. If you will recall, excises on ale, beer, aqua vitae, and strong waters were levied and annexed to the Crown by the 1695 Act for the Additional and Annexed Excises to replace the dissolved, annexed excise on malt. Under this 1696 Additional Excise Act, the annexed excises on alcoholic beverages shall be gradually increased in a two-year period.

From 1st March 1697 to 1st March 1698, 1s will be added to the 1695 prescribed rate for every pint of whisky and strong waters (additional levy applies to both malt and non-malt whisky/strong waters). Thus, in this 12-month period, the annexed excise on whisky and strong waters not made of malt shall be 3s (original rate) plus 1s (additional levy) for a total of 4s. Likewise, in the same 12-month period, the annexed excise on malt whisky and strong waters shall be 6s (original rate) plus 1s (additional levy) for a total of 7s.

From 1st March 1698 to 1st March 1699, on the other hand, the annexed excises levied by the 1695 Act of Parliament on whisky and strong waters shall increase by 3s. In the case of malt whisky and strong waters, therefore, the excise duties during this second 12-month period shall be 6s (original rate) plus 3s (additional levy) for a total of 9s. Likewise, in this 12-month increased-excise period, the excise duty on non-malt whisky and strong waters shall be the sum of 3s (original rate) and 3s (additional levy)—and this is 6s.

Union with England Act (1707)[21]

This is the Act ratifying and approving the Treaty of Union of the two Kingdoms of Scotland and England into the United Kingdom of Great Britain.

SOME REFERENCES TO AQUA VITAE OR WHISKY IN OLD SCOTLAND RECORDS

1494: Earliest known record of Scotch Whisky production is found in this year's Exchequer Rolls. The entry reads *"Eight bolls of malt to Friar John Cor wherewith to make aqua vitae."*

1498: An entry in this year's Accounts of the Lord High Treasurer of Scotland reads *"To the barbour that brocht aqua vitae to the King in Dundee ..."*

1505, 1st July: The Edinburgh Guild of Barber-Surgeons officially becomes the 10th Craft Guild recognized by the Edinburgh Town Council. The Guild is incorporated through the Seal of Clause and Charter of Privileges. One of the privileges specific to the Barber-Surgeons is the exclusive right to make and sell Scotch Whisky within Edinburgh.[22]

1506, 15th September: Accounts of the Lord High Treasurer for this day contain an entry *"Item, for aqua vite to the King."*[23]

1506, 16th September: Accounts of the Lord High Treasurer for this day contain an entry that reads, *"Item, for ane flacat of aqua vite to the King."*[24] This day, the King is back in Inverness after his trip to Tain.[25]

1506, 13th October: King James IV, through a Royal Charter, ratifies the Seal of Clause and Charter of Privileges initially awarded to the Edinburgh Guild of Barber-Surgeons in 1505 by the Edinburgh Town Council.[26] This confirms the Craft Guild's exclusive right to make and sell whisky.

1559: The book *Treasure of Evonymous* by Peter Morwyng is published. In this book, Morwyng talks about the thriving industry of distilling "burning water" or "aqua vit" from wine lees or "corrupt wine" and advances the opinion that there's nothing wrong with this practice (as cited in "The Art of Distillation," 1912).[27]

1603, 10th January: Records of Inverness for this day refer to a decree against someone named Thomas Makalley at the instance of someone called William Robertson for the price of 2 gallons aqua vitae.[28]

1611, 30th September: Inverness records for this day show statutes relevant to the sale of aqua vitae.[29]

1613, 25th January: Records of Inverness for this day contain references to certain brewers pursued for overcharging for ale and aqua vitae.[30]

1613: King James VI also ratifies the Edinburgh Guild of Barber-Surgeons' charter.[31]

1614, 8th July: Inverness records for this day refer to brewers overcharging for ale and aqua vitae.[32]

1618, 31st July: Inverness records for this day contain relevant aqua vitae statutes.[33]

1663, 25th May: Inverness records for this day contain an order regarding excise of aqua vitae.[34]

Endnotes

1 Scotch Whisky Association. *History*. Date accessed: October 29, 2011 (http://www.scotch-whisky.org.uk/swa/49.html).

2 Loch Lomond Distillery Co. Ltd. *A History of Scotch Whisky from Loch Lomond Distillers*. Date accessed: October 29, 2011 (http://www.lochlomonddistillery.com/history-of-scotch.htm).

3 Scotch Whisky Association. *History*. Date accessed: November 1, 2011 (http://www.scotch-whisky.org.uk/swa/49.html).

4 *The Records of the Parliaments of Scotland to 1707*, K.M. Brown et al., eds. (St Andrews, 2007-2011), A1552/2/13. Date accessed: November 4, 2011 (http://www.rps.ac.uk/trans/A1552/2/13).

5 *The Records of the Parliaments of Scotland to 1707*, K.M. Brown et al., eds. (St Andrews, 2007-2011), A1555/6/15. Date accessed: June 24, 2011 (http://www.rps.ac.uk/trans/A1555/6/15).

6 Statute Law: Papal Jurisdiction Act 1560. Date accessed: November 4, 2011 (http://www.legislation.gov.uk/aosp/1560/2).

7 *The Records of the Parliaments of Scotland to 1707*, K.M. Brown et al., eds. (St Andrews, 2007-2011), 1579/10/74. Date accessed: November 4, 2011 (http://www.rps.ac.uk/trans/1579/10/74).

8 *The Records of the Parliaments of Scotland to 1707*, K.M. Brown et al., eds. (St Andrews, 2007-2011), 1587/7/18. Date accessed: November 4, 2011 (http://www.rps.ac.uk/trans/1587/7/18).

9 *The Records of the Parliaments of Scotland to 1707*, K.M. Brown et al., eds. (St Andrews, 2007-2011), 1641/8/212. Date accessed: November 4, 2011 (http://www.rps.ac.uk/trans/1641/8/212).

10 *The Records of the Parliaments of Scotland to 1707*, K.M. Brown et al., eds. (St Andrews, 2007-2011), 1644/1/65. Date accessed: November 4, 2011 (http://www.rps.ac.uk/trans/1644/1/65).

11 *The Records of the Parliaments of Scotland to 1707*, K.M. Brown et al., eds. (St Andrews, 2007-2011), 1646/11/329. Date accessed: November 4, 2011 (http://www.rps.ac.uk/trans/1646/11/329).

12 *The Records of the Parliaments of Scotland to 1707*, K.M. Brown et al., eds. (St Andrews, 2007-2011), 1661/1/160. Date accessed: November 4, 2011 (http://www.rps.ac.uk/trans/1661/1/160).

13 *The Records of the Parliaments of Scotland to 1707*, K.M. Brown et al., eds. (St Andrews, 2007-2011), 1662/5/60. Date accessed: November 4, 2011 (http://www.rps.ac.uk/trans/1662/5/60).

14 *The Records of the Parliaments of Scotland to 1707*, K.M. Brown et al., eds. (St Andrews, 2007-2011), 1663/6/23. Date accessed: November 4, 2011 (http://www.rps.ac.uk/trans/1663/6/23).

15 The Free Dictionary by Farlex. *Mum - definition of mum by the Free Online Dictionary, Thesaurus and Encyclopedia.* Date accessed: December 23, 2011 (http://www.thefreedictionary.com/mum).

16 *The Records of the Parliaments of Scotland to 1707*, K.M. Brown et al., eds. (St Andrews, 2007-2011), 1681/7/32. Date accessed: November 4, 2011 (http://www.rps.ac.uk/trans/1681/7/32).

17 *The Records of the Parliaments of Scotland to 1707*, K.M. Brown et al., eds. (St Andrews, 2007-2011), 1685/4/16. Date accessed: November 4, 2011 (http://www.rps.ac.uk/trans/1685/4/16).

18 *The Records of the Parliaments of Scotland to 1707*, K.M. Brown et al., eds. (St And rews, 2007-2011), M1693/4/9. Date accessed: November 4, 2011 (http://www.rps.ac.uk/trans/M1693/4/9).

19 *The Records of the Parliaments of Scotland to 1707*, K.M. Brown et al., eds. (St Andrews, 2007-2011), 1695/5/187. Date accessed: November 4, 2011 (http://www.rps.ac.uk/trans/1695/5/187).

20 *The Records of the Parliaments of Scotland to 1707*, K.M. Brown et al., eds. (St Andrews, 2007-2011), 1696/9/54. Date accessed: November 4, 2011 (http://www.rps.ac.uk/trans/1696/9/54).

21 Union of England Act 1707. Date accessed: November 6, 2011 (http://www.legislation.gov.uk/aosp/1707/7).

22 Wade, Sir Henry. *The Barber Surgeons of Edinburgh - Thomas Vicary Lecture delivered at the Royal College of Surgeons of England.* (November 24, 1949). p. 358. Date accessed: June 7, 2011 (http://www.ncbi.nlm.nih.gov/pmc/articles/PMC2238401/pdf/annrcse00030-0005.pdf).

23 *Accounts of the Lord High Treasurer of Scotland = Compota thesaurariorum Regum Scotorum*, T. Dickson ed (Edinburgh: H.M. General Register House, 1877), p. 343. Date accessed: June 8, 2011 (http://www.archive.org/stream/accountsoflordhi03scot).

24 *Accounts of the Lord High Treasurer of Scotland = Compota thesaurariorum Regum Scotorum*, T. Dickson ed (Edinburgh: H.M. General Register House, 1877), p. 344. Date accessed: June 8, 2011 (http://www.archive.org/stream/accountsoflordhi03scot).

25 *Accounts of the Lord High Treasurer of Scotland = Compota thesaurariorum Regum Scotorum*, T. Dickson ed (Edinburgh: H.M. General Register House, 1877), p. 35. Date accessed: June 8, 2011 (http://www.archive.org/stream/accountsoflordhi03scot).

26 The Royal College of Surgeons of Edinburgh. *History.* Date accessed: November 4, 2011 (http://www.rcsed.ac.uk/site/360/default.aspx).

27 Wine Trade Club. *The Art of Distillation: a lecture delivered at Vintners' Hall.* (April 23, 1912). Date accessed: June 24, 2011 (http://www.archive.org/stream/artofdistillatio00winerich/artofdistillatio00winerich_djvu.txt).

28 Inverness (Scotland); Mackay, William, 1848-1928; Boyd, Herbert Cameron, 1868-; Laing, George Smith. *Records of Inverness.* (1911). p. 3. Date accessed: November 4, 2011 (http://www.archive.org/details/recordsofinverne02inveuoft).

29 Inverness (Scotland); Mackay, William, 1848-1928; Boyd, Herbert Cameron, 1868-; Laing, George Smith. *Records of Inverness.* (1911). p.84. Date accessed: June 7, 2011 (http://www.archive.org/details/recordsofinverne02inveuoft).

30 Inverness (Scotland); Mackay, William, 1848-1928; Boyd, Herbert Cameron, 1868-; Laing, George Smith. *Records of*

Inverness. (1911). p.102. Date accessed: June 7, 2011 (http://www.archive.org/details/recordsofinverne-02inveuoft).

31 McNee, Sir John. *Barber-Surgeons In Great Britain And Ireland - Thomas Vicary Lecture delivered at the Royal College of Surgeons of England.* (October 30, 1958). p.18. Date accessed: June 7, 2011 (http://www.ncbi.nlm.nih.gov/pmc/articles/PMC2413752/pdf/annrcse00345-0007.pdf).

32 Inverness (Scotland); Mackay, William, 1848-1928; Boyd, Herbert Cameron, 1868-; Laing, George Smith. *Records of Inverness.* (1911). p.122. Date accessed: June 7, 2011

(http://www.archive.org/details/recordsofinverne-02inveuoft).

33 Inverness (Scotland); Mackay, William, 1848-1928; Boyd, Herbert Cameron, 1868-; Laing, George Smith. *Records of Inverness.* (1911). p.154. Date accessed: June 7, 2011 (http://www.archive.org/details/recordsofinverne-02inveuoft).

34 Inverness (Scotland); Mackay, William, 1848-1928; Boyd, Herbert Cameron, 1868-; Laing, George Smith. *Records of Inverness.* (1911). p.215. Date accessed: June 7, 2011 (http://www.archive.org/details/recordsofinverne-02inveuoft).

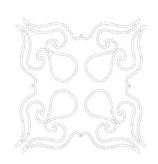

•Chapter III•

The Art of Distilling Single Malt Scotch Whisky

How is Single Malt Scotch made? This chapter gives you the answer. Here, I will discuss the art of distillation and the equipment, raw materials, and steps involved in the production of Single Malt Scotch Whisky.

DISTILLATION – HISTORY AND BASICS

Let's walk before we run. So before we advance to the art of distilling Single Malt Scotch, here is a brief introduction on the art of distillation.

What Is Distillation?

Distillation is a separation process used to break down a liquid mixture into its individual components according to such components' boiling points. It requires two processes: evaporation and condensation.

In distillation, the liquid mixture is heated to evaporate its individual components—one after the other according to their boiling points or volatility (i.e., their tendency to vaporize). The vapors are collected then cooled, so they will condense and turn into liquid— what is known as the distillate.

Old print depicting a distillation process

Distillation has several practical applications. It is used to purify compounds—i.e., separate the target component (e.g., water) from impurities. It is also used to break down a mixture into individual useful fractions—i.e., separate crude oil into usable fractions such as liquefied petroleum gas, butane, and diesel fuel to name a few. Those who make perfume also use distillation to isolate aromatic compounds.

In the case of alcoholic beverages, such as Single Malt Scotch Whisky, distillation is used to concentrate the ethanol content of fermented grains.

The History of Distillation

Distillation goes back a long way, but experts cannot agree on when this process was actually discovered.

On the one hand, there are claims that distillation is an ancient process and goes back to the earliest civilizations. A Mesopotamian cuneiform tablet, dated 2000 BC, contains a record of a woman named

Tapputi-Belatekallim, who allegedly used distillation to make perfume from a mixture of oleoresins, oils, and flowers.[1]

Distillation was also supposedly practiced during the period of antiquity (800 BC–200 BC). In 800 BC, the Chinese supposedly distilled spirits from rice beer.[2] Aristotle also touched on the subject of distillation in his work, "Meteorologica" (350 BC). Here, Aristotle discussed how sweet, drinkable water can be drawn out of salt water through evaporation. The exact passage read:

"Salt water when it turns into vapour becomes sweet, and the vapour does not form salt water when it condenses again. This I know by experiment."[3]

The fact remains, however, that the above-mentioned records are far from definite proof of distillation's ancient roots. For instance, there are concerns that what some scholars may have labeled as distilled spirits were not actually distillates in the true sense of the word.[4]

Let us put it this way. There is evidence that, before the Middle Ages, civilizations knew about the distillation process.

What is unclear is whether they applied this knowledge or, to be more precise, had the technology to *successfully* put it into practice. They might have tried to distill liquids, but there is no incontrovertible proof that they were able to produce distillates—and there lies the difficulty in proving the claim that ancient civilizations did practice and use distillation.

If we are going to use the existence of historical, verifiable records as a basis for establishing the origin of distillation as we know it, then the credit for inventing distillation belongs to the Alexandrian alchemists of the 2nd century AD. They had both the knowledge and the technology to distill liquids with a fair amount of success. They had distillation equipment, admittedly inefficient, that looked like the prototypes of a modern distillation apparatus.

The Arab alchemists followed in the Egyptian alchemists' footsteps and used distillation in their experiments (eighth century AD). There are those who say that the Arabs were the first to make distilled alcohol. However, the earliest

known record of alcohol distillation dates back to the twelfth century in Salerno, Italy.

So how did the art of distillation reach Scotland? According to the Scotch Whisky Association:

"The exact origins of distillation are lost in history, and nobody knows exactly when the art of distilling was first practised in Scotland."[5]

One famous version of Scottish distillation history involves St. Patrick himself bringing the art of distillation from Egypt to Ireland in the fifth century and, from Ireland, distillation knowledge supposedly spread to Scotland. However, there is little evidence to support this "legend." As mentioned in the preceding chapter, the earliest known record of alcohol distillation in Scotland can be found in the Exchequer Rolls of 1494.

SINGLE MALT SCOTCH DISTILLATION INGREDIENTS AND EQUIPMENT

Under this section, you will learn about the ingredients and the equipment used in the production of Single Malt Scotch Whisky.

Raw Materials

Single Malt Scotch Whisky has two basic ingredients: malted barley and water. During the production process, however, a distiller also needs yeast to initiate the fermentation of the mashed, malted barley. Plain caramel coloring may also be added to the Single Malt Scotch Whisky to improve its color before bottling.

Malted barley

Malted barley (also simply called "malt") is basically heat-dried, sprouted barley grains. Distilleries can make their own malt (in which case they are known as distiller maltsters) or they can source their malted barley from sales maltsters (maltsters that make malt for brewers, distilleries, and other entities that need malted barley).

Malted barley is made from whole barley grains. Whole barley grains are barley grains that have all three parts intact: the germ that—if the barley grain is allowed to germinate—will become the roots and shoots of the barley plant, the endosperm (which contains starch) that will fuel the growth of the germ, and the husk (the barley's outer shell) that protects the germ and the endosperm.

Water

Water is an essential part of the Single Malt Scotch Whisky production process. The quality and characteristics of the water a distillery uses affect the quality and characteristics of its Single Malt Scotch Whisky. Distillers carefully monitor their water sources and water transportation mechanisms/facilities, so they can control the quality of their whisky.

Water is used in several stages of the whisky production process:

- It is used for steeping barley grains during the malting process.
- It is mixed with the milled malted barley (i.e., grist) during the mashing process.
- It may be added to the freshly distilled spirit (produced during spirit still distillation) prior to casking.
- It may be added to mature Single Malt Scotch Whisky during the marrying process.
- It may be used to dilute the alcoholic strength of mature Single Malt Scotch Whisky prior to bottling.

Water is also used in pot still distillation, specifically in condensing alcoholic vapors leaving the pot still. In this case, however, water does not mix with the distillate.

• **Legal requirements**

According to the Scotch Whisky Regulations, distilleries must use water that will not change the nature of the whisky. The water must also be of a quality that conforms to the standards set forth in Council Directive 80/777/EEC (the natural mineral waters directive) and Council Directive 98/83/EC (the drinking water directive). In short, the water used in preparing Single Malt Scotch Whisky (or any other type of Scotch Whisky for that matter):

- should not contaminate the whisky,
- should be fit for human consumption as per the drinking water directive, and
- should meet the quality standards set forth in the natural mineral waters directive.

The water used in Scotch Whisky production must not be treated in ways other than those allowed in the natural mineral waters directive—i.e., "*the separation of its unstable elements, such as iron, manganese and sulphur compounds and certain undesirable constituents of a natural origin*" and "*the elimination or addition of carbon dioxide.*" However, the water used for whisky production—according to the Scotch Whisky Regulations—may be "*distilled, demineralized, permuted, or softened.*"

• **Water used in practice**

Scotch Whisky distilleries use only clean and unpolluted water in making their Scotch Whisky. They could do no less since the quality of their water affects the taste and flavor of their final product.

• *Flowing water*

Distilleries often use flowing water sources—e.g., rivers, constantly flowing lochs, burns, springs, boreholes. This ensures that their water sources are regularly replenished (i.e., will not become stagnant) and the water they are using is always fresh. In general, distilleries draw water from nearby bodies of water. For instance, Loch Lomond Distillery uses water sourced from the Loch Lomond water table. Typically, distilleries build their facilities in the area immediately around the water sources they intend to use in whisky production.

• *Water pipelines and storage tanks*

Distilleries usually draw water from their preferred water sources through a water pipeline. They draw water out only when needed; they may use water storage tanks, but distilleries do not use water that has been stored in a water storage tank or that has been in the water pipes too long. The fresher the water, the better it is for the quality of the whisky. Furthermore, distillers frequently sterilize/clean their tanks and pipes to ensure that these do not become breeding grounds for microorganisms and other contaminants that could impair water quality.

• *Hard or soft water*

Water used in making Single Malt Scotch Whisky may be soft or hard. Soft water is water that has minimal amounts of salts and minerals. The softness or hardness of water is determined by its source and its route to the surface; the quality of water that passes through granite will be different from the quality of water that passes over peaty deposits.

Distillers use soft or hard water according to their personal preferences. Distilleries that use soft water like it for the fact that it requires minimal processing. The minerals and salts in hard water can cause whisky clouding; this is undesirable if the object is to create clear and bright whisky. Such salts and

Stacked peat slabs

minerals, moreover, could dissolve or neutralize certain compounds that give whisky certain flavors and aromas.

However, there are distilleries that use hard water because they like the distinct flavors that the minerals and salts in this type of water give their finished product. Distilleries that use hard water simply soften their water to remove certain salts and minerals that can be harmful to the quality of their whisky.

• *Water temperature*

There are distillers that favor the use of cool water in their whisky production. Such distillers believe that the temperature of the water used affects the final quality of the whisky.

• *Peat content*

Finally, there are distillers that use only peaty water, especially for mashing and dilution. Peaty water is brownish water that has flowed over or passed through peaty soil and peat deposits.

Distillers that insist on using peaty water believe that peaty waters enhance the peaty flavors of or add peaty notes to their Single Malt Scotch Whisky. However, there are those that believe peaty water does not have enough peat content to add peaty flavors to whisky.[6]

Yeast

Distillers add yeast to the wort (the sugar-rich liquid produced

A "modern" stillhouse

after mashing milled malted barley) to start the fermentation process and brew the "beer" (the wash) that will be distilled in the first pot still distillation.

The yeast species that is most commonly used is *Saccharomyces cerevisiae*. Distillers often use varying strains of this species. The specific species of yeast, the specific strain or strains of yeast, and the quantity of yeast used—all have a direct bearing on the way the whisky will turn out. Thus, distilleries do not disclose such specific information to the public.

Plain caramel coloring

For cosmetic purposes, distilleries are permitted to add plain caramel coloring to Scotch Whisky prior to bottling. Plain caramel coloring is color E150a, which used to be known by the name "spirit caramel."

The Pot Still

A still is a distillation apparatus. As per the Scotch Whisky Regulations, the pot still is the only type of still that may be used when distilling Single Malt Scotch Whisky.

Material

Single Malt Scotch Whisky distilleries use copper pot stills. Copper is both the traditional and preferred pot still material for several reasons.

Copper has high thermal conductivity—i.e., it conducts heat very well. Thus, copper pot stills are very efficient at transferring heat from the heating source to the wash or low wines, and they are very efficient at transferring heat from the hot vapors to the cooling agent when it is time to convert these vapors to liquid.

Copper also has self-sanitizing properties. It is toxic to a wide variety of bacteria, fungi, algae, and other microorganisms. Thus, copper pot stills help incapacitate microbes that could contaminate the whisky.

Copper also helps neutralize sulfur-containing chemical compounds. Such compounds are produced during the fermentation of the mashed, malted barley; left alone, these compounds could cause undesirable characteristics in the whisky.

Types

Distilleries use two types of pot stills in the distillation of Single Malt Scotch Whisky: the wash still and the spirit still. The wash still is where the wash (also simply called beer) is distilled into low wines. The spirit still is where the low wines are distilled into the raw spirit that will be casked and matured to become Single Malt Scotch Whisky.

Design

The typical pot still is like a pot-bellied kettle with a neck and an arm. The bottom part of the pot still is like a deep and wide cauldron with a lid. The lid-like, upper half is connected to a neck that tapers upward. The neck is joined to a long, slender tube known as the Lyne Arm. The Lyne Arm, in turn, is connected to a condenser.

Pot still designs vary from one distillery to another. Some pot stills are very stout, some are less so. Some are very tall and some are quite short. Then there are pot stills with constricted necks, while some have reflux bowls, which look like ball joints, connecting the neck to the pot. The angle and length of the Lyne Arm also usually vary.

Heating mechanism

Pot stills are heated either directly or indirectly.

• Direct heating

In direct heating, fire is applied directly underneath the pot still. Pot stills that are heated through the use of fire are known as directly fired pot stills. To feed the flames, distillers use natural gas (although coal used to be the distillers' fuel of choice).

Unfortunately, direct firing can cause the incineration of solid particles deposited at the bottom of the pot, and this could cause unpleasant flavors in the resulting distillate. To prevent

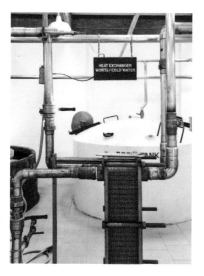

this, directly fired pot stills are outfitted with a rummager. The rummager rotates at a regular rate inside the pot still. As it rotates, its interlinked copper rings keep the liquid inside the pot moving so as to prevent the solid particles from adhering to the bottom of the pot where they could burn.

• Indirect heating

In indirect heating, superheated steam is generated in a water boiler fueled by oil or natural gas. The steam is then circulated inside the still via an internal heating coil or an internal heating cylinder.

In an *internal heating coil system*, the steam passes through a coiled pipe laid out at the bottom of the pot still. As the steam runs its spiral route, it loses its heat to the liquid inside the pot still until, at the end of the assembly, it turns back into water. It is then drawn out of the pot still and back to the boiler where it is reheated to become steam again.

In an *internal heating cylinder system*, several cylinders stand upright inside the pot still. The cylinders are open-ended so that the liquid inside the pot still could freely get in and out of the heating cylinders. The cylinders have hollow walls within which steam is circulated. Intake tubes connected to the cylinders from the top feed steam into the hollow cylinder walls. As steam goes down the closed cylinder walls, the steam loses its heat to the liquid inside the cylinders. After circulating through the hollow cylinder walls, the steam becomes water, which is drawn out through exit tubes and fed back into the boiler for reheating.

Compared to direct firing, indirect heating causes less scorching. However, this problem is not totally eliminated, especially in internal heating coil systems where solid particles may still stick to the steam coils.

Cooling mechanism

The condenser is the apparatus that converts vapors into liquid. A pot still condenser is made up of two parts: the inner pipe coil (also known as the worm) and the water tank in which the inner pipe coil is immersed.

The inner pipe coil is made of copper for efficient heat conduction. As the vapors from the Lyne Arm pass through to the inner pipe coil of the condenser, they gradually lose their heat to the water in the water tank, so that at the end of their inner pipe coil cycle, the vapors become liquid—the distillate.

Oak Casks

The casks used for aging whisky are usually made from ei-

ther American white oak (*Quercus alba*) or European oak. They can be new, but Scotch Whisky distillers mostly use second-hand or used casks. Distillers also often re-use their oak casks. To prepare a used cask for refilling or re-using, the distiller toasts or chars the inner surface of the cask for a few minutes; this process reactivates the oak's tannins.

Distillers buy used oak casks from wineries and other distilleries. Typically, these second-hand casks used to hold (for storage or aging purposes) the following wines and other spirits:

- Sherry (fortified wine from Jerez, Spain)
- Port (fortified wine from the Douro Valley of Portugal)
- Madeira (fortified wine from the Madeira Islands, Portugal)
- Bordeaux (wine from the Bordeaux wine region)
- Cognac (grape brandy from the Cognac appellation in France)
- Calvados (apple brandy from the Calvados appellation in France)

- Bourbon (corn whiskey from the USA)

According to the Scotch Whisky Regulations, Scotch Whisky must be aged in oak casks with a capacity that does not exceed 700 liters (184.92 US gallons). The following are the most common types of oak casks used in Scotch Whisky distillation:

- oak octaves – hold approximately 50 liters / 13.21 US gallons
- oak quarters – hold approximately 125 liters / 33.02 US gallons
- oak barrels – hold approximately 175 liters / 46.23 US gallons
- oak hogsheads – hold approximately 250 liters / 66.04 US gallons
- oak butts – hold approximately 500 liters / 132.09 US gallons

THE BARLEY'S JOURNEY: FROM BARLEY TO SINGLE MALT SCOTCH WHISKY

Now comes the good part. In this section, you will learn about the specific steps involved in making Single Malt

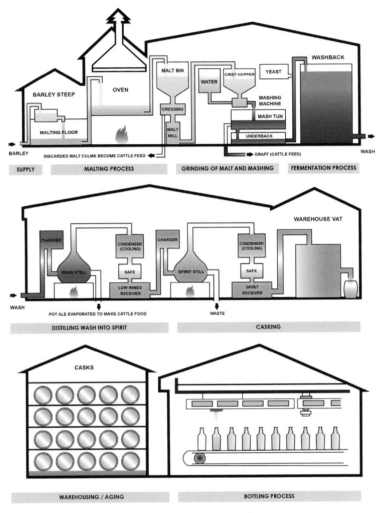

This diagram represents the complete Whisky making process.

Scotch Whisky. Read on and follow the journey of the barley as it becomes malt, which is then combined with water to become Single Malt Scotch Whisky.

Phase One
– Barley to Wash

Barley

Maltsters (which, as mentioned earlier, can be distiller maltsters or sales maltsters) get their whole barley grains from barley growers. After receiving their supply of barley grains, they gently and immediately dry the grains to ensure minimal moisture content.

This drying process temporarily halts the natural tendency of the barley germ to sprout or germinate. Thus, newly dried barley grains cannot be immediately malted. They must be allowed to rest for around six weeks or more until the germ has overcome its dormancy.

After the grains have been stored for the required length of time, they undergo careful inspection. Maltsters select evenly sized grains. The grains' husks should be intact and not broken or skinned. They should also have the required moisture content.

The grains that pass the maltsters' inspection are then cleaned in preparation for the next step in the malting process.

Barley steep

The carefully screened barley grains are steeped or immersed in water to raise their moisture content; this is to prepare the grains for their next stop—the malting floor.

Water steeping is a multi-stage, systematic, and carefully controlled procedure that can last from 1 ½ to 2 ½ days. The water used must be rich in oxygen. Barley grains need oxygen to germinate, and they will leech this oxygen off the water while they are immersed in it.

As the barley grains start germinating, they produce carbon dioxide, which could inhibit the grains' further development. It is for this reason that the steeping water is changed a few times throughout the course of the water steeping stage. After every immersion, the water is drained out and the barley grains are exposed to air.

The amount of water used in steeping and the amount of time the barley grains are aerated after every immersion are precisely measured and controlled to ensure that, at the end of the steeping stage, the grains will have just the right amount of moisture (around 46%) for optimal germ development.

Malting floor

After water steeping, the moist barley grains are transferred to

Malting floor

and laid out evenly on a germination vessel: the malting floor (for floor malting), the rotating malting drum (for drum malting), or the malting box (for box malting).

Germination is important; it is during this stage that the starch in the endosperm is gradually converted to sugar to fuel the growth of the germ. Germination increases the barley grains' sugar content. If the barley grains are not germinated, they will not be as readily fermentable.

The germinating barley grains (called green malt) will stay in the germination vessel for however long it takes them to achieve the maltster's desired germ development. In general, barley grains stay in the germination vessel for around four to six days, but some distilleries let the grains germinate for more than one week.

During the germination stage, the barley must be continuously aerated to ensure that all of the grains will develop or germinate at an even rate. During the germination process, humidity levels are also carefully controlled to ensure that the germinating grains will not dry out, and the germination will not stop before the grains are completely ready.

• Floor malting

In floor malting, a large floor space is the maltsters' germination vessel of choice. Maltsters layer out the grains on the floor according to their desired thickness. To aerate the grains and dissipate the heat produced by the grains as they germinate, the barley grains are turned regularly using manually operated or automated wooden paddles.

• Drum malting

In drum malting, maltsters transfer the moist barley grains into large germination drums. These drums rotate continuously but very gently to help disperse the heat produced during germination and encourage the flow of air among the grains.

• Box malting

In box malting, maltsters spread out the moist grains (around 4-feet deep) inside the malting box (e.g., Saladin box). The malting box can be rectangular or circular. It can be made of concrete or bricks, and it may also be lined with steel. To aerate the grains and keep them moist, humid air is blown into the box through the perforated floor. Exhaust fans are used to disperse the heat produced by the germinating grains.

To ensure the even development of the barley grains in the malting box, the grains are regularly turned (i.e., grains are moved from the bottom to the top and vice versa) by slow-moving, rotating, screw-like turners. In a rectangular malting box, these mechanical turners are anchored on side railings, so they can move up and down the length of the box. In a circular malting box, the screw-like turners are arrayed radially from a central arm, which rotates on its axis to move the turners along in a circular path.

Malt kiln

Once the desired amount of germination has been attained (that is to say, once the grains have optimal sugar content), the green malt is moved—nor-

A peat fired Malt Kiln

mally through an automated process—to the malt kiln or malt oven where heated air is used to dry and cure the barley grains. It is during this drying stage that green malt is transformed into malted barley.

The traditional malt kiln or oven is shaped like a multi-level tower. At the base is a furnace for the fire. Above that is a chamber, where the air blown into the malt kiln is heated. The hot air in this air chamber rises to penetrate the next level, where the barley grains are located. To control the inflow of air into the oven and the outflow of moisture evaporating from the grains, the malt kiln is also outfitted with fans and flues that can be opened and closed as needed.

Traditionally, distilleries used peat fires in their malt kiln furnaces. Today natural gas, which is a cleaner fuel than peat, is the fuel of choice of most distilleries.

However, the shift from peat to natural gas fuel in the malt kilning process has a downside. When peat burns, it gives off a thick, pungent smoke that deeply permeates the barley grains drying in the malt kiln. This is what gives malted barley—and the Single Malt Scotch Whisky made from it—its characteristically peaty flavor.

The use of natural gas, therefore, means the loss of a significant amount of peaty flavors. As a compromise, distillers still often burn peat while the malt is drying in the oven. However, peat is not the energy source; it is burned only to produce peaty smoke, which is blown into the chamber where the green malt is drying. This ensures that the resulting malted barley will have a flavor profile similar to that of peat-dried malt.

The drying stage is a two-phase process. First comes the *initial drying phase*, done to drastically reduce the grains' moisture content. During this initial drying phase, the temperature inside the malt oven is maintained at around 35–38 °C and the air flow is kept at a maximum. Next comes the *curing stage*, done to arrest further germ development (i.e., lock in the grains at their current level of germination). As the barley grains enter the curing stage, the temperature inside the malt oven is gradually increased, and the air flow gradually decreased.

After the drying and curing stages, the barley grains may undergo additional processing (e.g., roasting, toasting) if the maltster wants to produce special malts.

Malt bin

After leaving the malt kiln, the dried malted barley grains are stockpiled and allowed to cool in the malt bin in preparation for the next step—dressing.

Dressing

The dried and cured grains are removed from the malt bin and transferred to the malt deculming machine for dressing. At this stage, the rootlets that have formed on the grains during the germination stage (these rootlets are known as culms) are trimmed off and removed by the deculming machine. Maltsters collect these culms, which have high protein content, and sell them to livestock growers as animal feed.

After deculming, the malted barley grains are stored for a while before they are sent to distillers or before they are milled (if the distiller made his own malted barley). It is recommended that malted barley be stored for a minimum of two weeks after kilning.[7] This resting/storage period gives the grains sufficient time to recover from kilning-induced dormancy.

Malt mill

When the distillers are ready to turn their malt to Single Malt Scotch Whisky, they take the dressed malt out of storage for milling. Malted barley grains are milled to turn them into grist. The grist has high sugar content, and it has the appearance and consistency of flour.

Note: As earlier mentioned, distillers may choose not to produce their own malt; if they choose to go this route, they can buy malt from a malt supplier (i.e., a sales maltster). Even so, distillers who outsource their malt still usually do their milling in-house.

Grist hopper

The grist is taken to the grist hopper. This is a container located above the mashing machine, and it holds the milled grains until they are ready for mashing.

Mashing water tank

Also located above the mashing machine, this tank holds the water that will be used for mashing the grist.

Mashing machine

Grist from the grist hopper and hot water from the mashing water tank flow into the mashing machine, where the grist and the water are combined at exact proportions. The water is not dumped into the grist in one shot; it is added in stages, and the temperature of the mixture gradually increases with every addition. The combination of water and grist produces a porridge-like substance known as the mash.

A mash tun in action

Mash tun

The mash flows from the mashing machine and into the mash tun below. The mash tun is an insulated metal tub, outfitted with automated, metal rakes to stir the mash. It is also heated to ensure that the optimal temperature for sugar extraction can be maintained.

In the mash tun, sugars from the grist are transferred to the water. This process produces a sugar-rich liquid known as the wort.

Underback

Once it has the desired concentration of sugars, the wort is allowed to flow out of the mash tun and into the underback. The spent barley grains (i.e., draff) remaining in the mash tun are also collected; distilleries sell them to livestock growers who use the draff as cattle feed.

In the underback, the wort is left alone to cool. After it has cooled down sufficiently (around 23 °C), it is allowed to flow into the washback for further processing.

Yeast

Yeast is combined with the wort in the washback; it is yeast that facilitates the fermentation of the wort.

Washback

In the washback, the mixture of wort and yeast is allowed to ferment for a few days (usually two to five days). During this period, the yeast consumes the sugars in the wort, producing alcohol as a by product.

The end product of the fermentation process is a weakly alcoholic beer of around 8% Alcohol by Volume (ABV). This is known as the wash, which is the feedstock or the raw material used in wash still distillation.

Note: For the sake of accuracy, it must be noted that the wash is not the end product of fermentation. The wash is technically the mixture of wort and yeast; so the moment yeast is added to the wort, the wort immediately turns into wash.[8] However, in this book, we will use the term "wash" the way it is commonly understood—as the fermented wort.

Phase Two – Wash to Spirit

Wash charger

The wash (i.e., fermented wort) from the washback flows into and is collected in the charger. This particular charger is connected to the wash still, and it holds the wash in preparation for the next step.

Wash still

The wash from the wash charger is fed into the wash still and heated. Since alcohol is more volatile than water, the alcohol content is vaporized first.

The vapors from the pot rise into the neck of the still and into the Lyne Arm. From there they are channeled into the condenser where they are turned back into liquid. Since the first vapors to rise in the pot have the highest alcoholic strength, the first distillate fractions are strongly alcoholic. As the distillation progresses, the alcohol by volume content of the distillate gradually decreases until it reaches zero.

Wash still distillation typically takes more than four hours, and it ends when no more alcohol can be distilled from the wash. The alcoholic distillate produced during wash still distillation is known as low wines. The remaining non-alcoholic wash in the pot, called pot ale, is drained out; it may be evaporated so that the solid residues can be sold as animal feed.

Safe

The stream of distillate leaving the condenser is directed toward the spirit safe, where it is carefully assessed by the stillman (the

specialist manning the pot still) to ensure that only alcoholic distillate will be collected and saved for further processing.

Low wines receiver

Alcoholic distillate, after passing through the spirit safe, flows into the low wines receiver where it stays until it is needed for the next step.

Low wines charger

When the stillman is ready to continue distillation, low wines are allowed to flow from the low wines receiver into the spirit still charger.

Spirit still

To initiate spirit still distillation, low wines from the charger are fed into the spirit still and heated. Just like in wash still distillation, vapors rise to the neck of the pot, into the Lyne Arm and into the condenser where they turn to liquid.

Spirit still distillation produces a stream of liquid spirit known as the spirit run. Spirit still distillation ends when the stream of distillate's ABV reaches zero. The liquid remaining inside the pot

at this point (known as spent lees) is drained out; like pot ale, spent lees can be evaporated and turned into animal feed.

Safe

Just like the alcoholic distillate produced in wash still distillation, the alcoholic strength of the spirit still distillate decreases as the distillation progresses. Thus, the stillman runs the stream of distillate through the spirit safe, so he can assess the distillate and divide it into three fractions based on alcoholic strength.

The *first fraction*, called first cut or foreshot (also heads), comes out of the pot still first. This fraction is extremely alcoholic and full of impurities. Since it cannot be used in its present form, the stillman directs it to a foreshot receiver, where it stays until it can be added to the next batch of low wines.

The *third fraction*, called third cut or feints (also tails), comes out of the pot still last. This is the least alcoholic fraction. This, like the foreshot, is directed to the feints receiver, so it can be added to the next batch of low wines.

The *second fraction*, called middle cut or heart of the run, comes out of the pot still second. This has the desired alcoholic strength and compounds that will imbue whisky with unique characteristics. It is this portion of the spirit run that is in readily usable form. This fraction, the stillman directs to the spirit receiver.

Note: The middle cut's specific alcoholic strength varies from one distillery to another. Choosing how to cut the distillate fractions is a distiller's prerogative. In Glen Scotia, the middle cut begins at 72% ABV and ends at 63% ABV.[9]

Spirit receiver

As mentioned earlier, the middle cut or the second fraction of the spirit run is allowed to flow from the spirit safe into the spirit receiver. Here it will stay until it is ready for the warehouse vat.

Warehouse vat

After the distiller has made a detailed accounting of the spirit produced during spirit still distillation and collected in the spirit receiver, the spirit is transferred to the warehouse vat. There it will stay until the distiller is ready to start casking.

Cask

Oak casks are filled with freshly distilled spirit from spirit vats. The spirit from the vats may or may not be diluted prior to casking; it all depends on the distiller's preferences. At this point, the spirit in the casks

looks, smells, and tastes nothing like what it will look, smell, and taste like after it has been properly aged.

After filling up the oak casks with raw spirit, the distiller transports these casks to an excise warehouse or to any other storage location regulated by Her Majesty's Revenue and Customs. There they will stay until the distiller has decided that the spirit they contain has undergone sufficient aging.

Phase Three – Spirit to Scotch Whisky

As per the Scotch Whisky Regulations, raw whisky must age in oak casks for at least three years before it can legally become Scotch Whisky. However, distilleries normally age their whisky for longer than three years. It is common for Single Malt Scotch Whiskies to be aged for twelve years or longer.

Oak maturation is a crucial phase in the production of Single Malt Scotch Whisky. The wood of the oak casks, particularly the toasted or charred inner surfaces that

come in contact with the spirit, greatly influences and improves the quality of Scotch Whisky.

First, it removes undesirable compounds and flavors from the raw spirit. Second, it adds unique flavors to the whisky; through the years, the oak passes on certain compounds to the maturing whisky. Third, some of the compounds extracted from the wood interact with some of the compounds in the whisky, and this creates new flavors and aromas.

Many factors influence the development of the Single Malt Scotch Whisky during its oak maturation phase. The following are a few of these factors:

- *The length of time the Single Malt Scotch Whisky is aged.*
The longer the aging period, the longer time the whisky has to interact with the oak.

- *The size/capacity of the oak cask.*
The smaller the cask, the more interaction there is between the wood and the Single Malt Scotch Whisky. The use of smaller casks can therefore accelerate the oak maturation process.

- *The number of times the cask has been used.*

Single Malt Scotch Whiskies matured in brand new oak casks typically gain the strongest oak flavors. This is true even in the case of casks that used to hold a different alcoholic beverage. Thus, the first batch of Single Malt Scotch Whisky aged in a used cask (the first filling) will extract a greater amount of flavor from this cask than the second batch of whisky aged in the same cask (the second filling).

- *If using a second-hand cask, the type of beverage the cask used to hold.*

A used Bordeaux wine cask will influence a Single Malt Scotch Whisky differently than a used Sherry cask. Distilleries may take advantage of this by "finishing" a Single Malt Scotch Whisky—that is, transferring it from the oak cask where it has been aging for years into a different cask and letting it rest there for a period of a few months or even years.

- *The location of the warehouse.* Oak casks are porous, so the quality of the surrounding air can affect the maturing whisky. Thus, Single Malt Scotch Whisky that has been allowed to mature in a coastal warehouse has flavors distinct from

Single Malt Scotch Whisky that has been allowed to mature in an inland warehouse.

Phase Four
– Processing Prior
to Bottling

The whisky production process does not always end with maturation. The following are some of the preparations that a Single Malt Scotch Whisky could go through before it is bottled and sold.

Marrying

A bottle of Single Malt Scotch Whisky can contain whisky that is a blend of single malts from different casks. To achieve harmony among the chosen malts, the distillery can blend or vat together Single Malt Scotch Whiskies from different casks. The mixture of single malts is then allowed to rest for several months. This process of blending then vatting together Single Malt Scotch Whiskies from different casks is known as "marrying" the whisky.

Marrying lets distilleries come up with products that exhibit consistent characteristics whatever the year of bottling.

Dilution with water

Casked Single Malt Scotch Whisky is typically at more than 60% ABV. Therefore, distilleries often dilute their whisky with water before bottling. Single Malt Scotch Whisky is usually bottled at 40–46% ABV.

However, water dilution is not required. Some distillers choose to bottle at cask strength, especially for really old Single Malt Scotch Whisky. Distilleries also set their own bottling ABV thresholds and ceilings.

Dilution is usually done before bottling. In some distilleries, however, dilution is done in two stages: during the marriage of malts and prior to bottling.

Filtering

Distilleries can let their Single Malt Scotch Whisky pass through depth filter sheets (made of cellulose fiber impregnated with shells). This is done to clarify and brighten the whisky before it is bottled and sold.

Filtration may be performed at ambient temperature or at chilled conditions. Filtering at ambient temperatures is done mainly to remove fine char (from oak casks), fibers, and other solid particles that are muddying up the Single Malt Scotch Whisky. Filtering at chilled conditions, known as chill filtering, is done to remove haziness or cloudiness caused by oils, fats, and other compounds.

• **Chill filtering**

Water dilution causes the Single Malt Scotch Whisky to cloud up or haze up. The addition of water disturbs the balance in the whisky; some of the compounds trapped in alcohol are freed after dilution, causing visible cloudiness.

Chill filtering is the remedy to haziness caused by water dilution. To perform chill filtering, whisky is first chilled to a temperature of around 0 °C (actual chilling temperatures vary from one distillery to another) before it is passed through filter sheets. The cold temperature causes the oils, fats, and other compounds to gather into bigger clumps, making them easier to filter out or remove.

Chill filtering also helps distilleries prevent chill haze or the clouding up of whisky when it is transported to a colder country or stored in cold conditions for an extended period of time. Finally, chill filtering removes the risk that the Single Malt Scotch Whisky will cloud up when the end consumer adds water or ice to it.

However, chill filtering has a downside. Some of the compounds it strips off are the very flavor compounds that distillers have worked so hard to develop in their whisky. Thus, some distillers would rather risk chill haze than perform chill filtration. Other distillers simply choose to bottle their whisky at an ABV of 46% or higher; at such alcoholic strength, whisky is less prone to chill haze as well as cloudiness when water or ice is added.

Endnotes

1   Tapputi. (2011, May 10). In *Wikipedia, The Free Encyclopedia*. Date accessed: July 3, 2011 (http://en.wikipedia.org/w/index.php?title=Tapputi&oldid=428466482).

2   Distilled spirit. (2011). In *Encyclopædia Britannica online*. Date accessed: June 25, 2011 (http://www.britannica.com/EBchecked/topic/166115/distilled-spirit).

3   Aristotle. (350 B.C.). *Meteorology*. (E. W. Webster, Trans). Date accessed: June 25, 2011 (http://classics.mit.edu/Aristotle/meteorology.2.ii.html).

4   Forbes, Robert James. (1970). *A short history of the art of distillation: from the beginnings up to the death of Cellier Blumenthal*. p 3. Date accessed: July 3, 2011 (http://books.google.com/books?id=Xeq WOkKYn28C&printsec=fron ver#v=onepage&q&f=false).

5   Scotch Whisky Association. (n.d.). *History*. Date accessed: July 3, 2011 (http://www.scotch-whisky.org.uk/swa/49.html).

6   The Whisky Store. (n.d.). *Peat and its meaning for whisky*. Date accessed: July 10, 2011 (http://www.whisky.de/archiv/experts/peat.htm).

7   *Handbook of Brewing: Processes, Technology, Markets*, H. M. Eßlinger ed. p. 157. Date accessed: January 15, 2012 (http://books.google.com.ph/books?id=8ppgs-BEG_8C).

8   Scotch Whisky Association. (n.d.). *FAQs*. Date accessed: July 8, 2011 (http://www.scotch-whisky.org.uk/swa/93.html#Wash).

9   Glen Scotia Distillery. (n.d.) *Distilling the Spirit*. Date accessed: January 16, 2012 (http://www.glenscotia-distillery.co.uk/distillation.html).

•Chapter IV•

How to Drink Single Malt Scotch Whisky

Is there really a proper way of drinking Single Malt Scotch Whisky? Yes, you can "just sip it." That will work, but only if your goal is to get the whisky from your glass down your throat and into your stomach as soon as possible.

Now, if your goal is to enjoy your Single Malt Scotch Whisky to the fullest, to get to know its aromas and flavors (specifically, to assess all of its organoleptic properties - i.e., its characteristics as determined by your senses), and to grow your appreciation for this one-of-a-

kind spirit, "just sipping it" will not cut it.

Read this chapter to learn about Scotch Whisky etiquette and the technique I use when tasting Single Malt Scotch. In this chapter, I have also included the Scotch Whisky Research Institute's Flavour Wheel to help you describe Scotch Whisky's aromas and flavors. You will find this very useful if you want to review a Single Malt Scotch Whisky or if you intend to write your own whisky tasting notes.

Note: This whisky tasting guide applies not only to Single Malt

Scotch Whisky but to whisky in general.

TASTING TECHNIQUE

In this section, we will learn about what your senses can tell you about a Single Malt Scotch Whisky, the most common aromas found in Scotch Whisky, and the step-by-step procedures for and tips on tasting a Single Malt Scotch Whisky.

Tasting with Your Senses

Tasting Single Malt Scotch Whisky is not just about using your tongue. It is like tasting wine in that it involves almost all of your senses. Professional whisky tasters use their sense of sight, sense of smell, sense of touch, and sense of taste when "tasting" a Single Malt Scotch. Thus, after a tasting, you should be able to describe the complete organoleptic profile of the Single Malt Scotch Whisky you have just tasted; in other words, you should know not only what the Single Malt Scotch tastes like but also what it looks like, what it smells like, and what it feels like.

Sight

What does the Single Malt Scotch Whisky look like? Use your sense of sight to assess the whisky's color, viscosity, and clarity. These are the visual clues that experienced tasters use to draw conclusions about a whisky's age and the production process it has undergone.

• **Color**

The color of the Single Malt Scotch Whisky can provide information on the type of oak cask used for aging and the age of the whisky.

Freshly distilled malt whisky (also known as new-make or raw Single Malt Scotch Whisky) is the color of gin or vodka. It is the aging process that gives Single Malt Scotch Whisky its color. Specifically, it is prolonged contact with the oak cask used for aging that gives mature whisky its copper amber color.

Thus, if the distiller did not add plain caramel coloring to the Single Malt Scotch Whisky prior to bottling, the color of the whisky would help you determine:

- The type of oak used (e.g., European, American white oak)

As a general rule, oak casks made of American white oak impart less color to whisky than oak casks made of European oak.

- The length of time the whisky has spent aging in the oak cask

The color of whisky deepens with time. The longer whisky stays in an oak cask, the more color it gains from the wood.

- The alcoholic beverage the oak cask used to hold (e.g., wine, Sherry, Bourbon) if the cask is second-hand

Scotch distillers typically use second-hand oak casks. These casks used to hold other alcoholic beverages like Sherry, Bourbon, and red wine, to name a few. The type of beverage previously stored in the oak cask used for aging whisky influences the whisky's color.

A yellow, honey, or golden color usually indicates aging in an oak cask that used to hold Bourbon, while a dark amber or copper color usually indicates aging in an oak cask that used to hold Sherry. A darker red color, on the other hand, usually indicates aging in an oak cask that used to hold Port.

- The number of times the cask has been filled

Distillers often reuse their oak casks. They reuse not only virgin oak casks but also second-hand casks or those that used to hold alcoholic beverages other than Scotch.

This practice of refilling oak casks has a distinct effect on the color of Single Malt Scotch Whisky. As a general rule, the greater the number of times an oak cask is filled, the less its influence on the color of the whisky.

Thus, a Single Malt Scotch Whisky aged in a refilled Sherry cask usually has a light chestnut color, whereas a Single Malt Scotch Whisky aged in a first-fill Sherry cask (i.e., a Sherry cask filled with new-make Single Malt Scotch for the first time) is usually auburn or the color of mahogany. Likewise, a Single Malt Scotch Whisky aged in a first-fill Bourbon cask is usually more golden than a Single Malt Scotch Whisky aged in a refilled Bourbon cask.

Proceed with caution when using color as a basis for forming conclusions on the length of time a Single Malt Scotch Whisky has been aged and the type of oak cask in which it has been aged. You should consider all the possibilities. For instance, a mahogany color usually means that the Single Malt Scotch Whisky has been aged in a first-fill Sherry cask, but it can also mean that the whisky has been aged in a thrice-filled Port cask (thus the lighter reddish color) or that it has been aged for a long time in a refilled Sherry cask (thus the darker color).

Viscosity: Here you can see the tears, also known as legs, dripping down the glass.

• Viscosity

Viscosity can provide information on the age and alcoholic strength of the whisky.

Viscosity is the thickness or thinness of the whisky. As a general rule, older whiskies tend to be thicker than younger whiskies. Whiskies with a higher alcoholic strength also tend to be thicker than whiskies with a lower alcoholic strength.

• Clarity or brightness

The clarity or brightness of the Single Malt Scotch Whisky can give you information on whether or not the whisky has undergone chill filtration.

Single Malt Scotch Whisky is usually diluted before it is bottled, but this disturbs the balance in the whisky by releasing some of the oily and fatty compounds previously trapped in alcohol into the whisky's water content. Since these newly released compounds are insoluble in water, they cause the whisky to cloud up or haze up.

Hazy or cloudy whisky can be off-putting to some consumers. Some distillers also prefer to bottle only clear and bright whisky. For these reasons, some distillers chill-filter their Single Malt Scotch Whisky after water dilution and before bottling.

Chill filtering involves chilling the whisky to a temperature of plus or minus 0 °C then passing it through a depth filter. Chilling causes the suspended oily and fatty compounds to clump up. The bigger size of the oily and fatty compounds in chilled whisky makes them easier to filter out when the whisky is passed through filtering sheets. After chill filtering, the whisky becomes clear and bright once more—just as clear and bright as it was before water dilution.

Unfortunately, some of the compounds filtered out during chill filtration are actually the very compounds that give Single Malt Scotch Whisky their unique character and flavor.

By assessing its clarity and brightness, you may be able to tell whether or not a Single Malt Scotch Whisky has been chill-filtered. Of course, you can also simply check the label since distillers often include chill filtering information on their whisky bottles—but that is just not as fun as trying to guess through visual cues alone whether the Scotch has been chill-filtered or not.

A Single Malt Scotch Whisky that has not been chill-filtered could cloud up or haze up when water is added. Thus, experienced whisky tasters often add a little water to their whisky before assessing its brightness or clarity.

Unchill-filtered whisky is also more likely to develop chill haze (cloudiness caused by the cold) than chill-filtered whisky. Whisky usually exhibits visible signs of chill haze in very low temperatures (temperatures near 0°C). The lower the temperature, the less soluble some of the compounds in the whisky become. These compounds are less likely to stay dissolved in the whisky; when they come out of the solution, they cloud up the whisky. Therefore, if you live in a cold climate or if you keep your whisky in cold storage, you may not even have to add water before you can venture a guess on whether or not the whisky has been chill-filtered.

Note: You must consider alcoholic strength before concluding that a bright and clear Single Malt Scotch Whisky has been chill-filtered. Unchill-filtered Single Malt Scotch Whiskies with high alcohol content (usually 46% Alcohol-by-Volume) generally remain visibly bright and clear even after slight dilution and slight chilling. Unchill-filtered Single Malt Scotch Whiskies with a high ABV can still haze up, of course, but it usually takes more water and a bigger drop in temperature to do this—certainly more dilution and chilling than is needed to haze up low-ABV, unchill-filtered whiskies.

Smell

What does the whisky smell like? Use your sense of smell to assess the whisky's aromas and flavors while it is in the glass, while it is in your mouth, and after you have swallowed the whisky. The aromas and flavors of a Single Malt Scotch Whisky may be used as a basis when trying to guess its region and distillery of origin.

• Geography and aromas/flavors

Geography is one of the main determinants of the aromas you will find in a Single Malt Scotch Whisky. Specific geographical factors include temperature, microclimate, air quality, soil quality, proximity to the sea, and altitude. These factors have a direct influence on the quality of the ingredients (specifically the malted barley, the water, and the yeast) and the aging process both of which, in turn, have a direct influence on the aromas that the Single Malt Scotch Whisky will ultimately develop.

Note, however, that aromas cannot be used as your sole basis for pinpointing the region of origin. As explained above, it is not the region of origin *per se*, but specific geographical factors that have an indirect influence on the aromatic and flavor profile of a Single Malt Scotch Whisky.

Thus, two distilleries from different production regions can produce whiskies with similar aromas and flavors if they are subject to the same geographical conditions. Likewise, two neighboring distilleries from the same Scotch Whisky production region can produce whiskies with significantly distinct aromas and flavors if they are subject to different geographical conditions.

It should also be noted that geographical factors are just part of the equation that determines the aromas of a Single Malt Scotch Whisky. Specific production processes are some of the other factors that have an effect on the aromatic and flavor profile of whisky. Thus, two neighboring distilleries that are subject to similar geographical conditions can produce Single Malt Scotch Whiskies with markedly distinct aromas and flavors if they use significantly different production methods.

That being said, the fact remains that knowing how to identify the aromas and flavors of a Single Malt Scotch Whisky can be very useful in whisky tastings. With prac-

tice and experience, a time will come when you can identify a Single Malt Scotch Whisky—its production region and distillery of origin—based on its aromas and flavors alone.

• **Aromas and flavors: what is the difference?**

The following are examples of the aromas and flavors you may encounter when tasting Single Malt Scotch Whiskies:

- peaty
- smoky
- grassy
- leafy
- fruity
- floral
- medicinal
- sweet
- cereal

There are a lot more aromas and flavors than these. Familiarize yourself with the most common aromas and flavors found in Scotch Whisky by using the Scotch Whisky Research Institute's Flavour Wheel included in the latter part of this chapter.

Aromas are the scents or fragrances that you detect

through the nasal cavity (i.e., nose). The process of detecting aromas through the nose (or to be more precise, through the nostrils) is known as orthonasal olfaction.

To detect the aromas of Single Malt Scotch Whisky, you put the snifter of whisky under your nose and sniff it. The scent or odor molecules from the whisky will then bind themselves to specific olfactory receptors in your nose. This triggers a reaction and the scent information is sent to your brain, specifically to the olfactory bulb in the limbic system. There, the perceived odors or aromas are "identified" by matching them with the existing scents in your brain's olfactory or scent memory.

Flavors, on the other hand, are just like aromas in that they are also scents and fragrances. However, they are detected through the oral cavity (i.e., mouth). The process of detecting aromas through the mouth is known as retronasal olfaction.

To detect the flavors of a Single Malt Scotch Whisky, you sip a small amount of whisky and swirl it inside your mouth. When the whisky comes in contact with the warmth of your mouth and saliva, previously trapped scent molecules are released. These odor molecules will then travel through the retronasal passage (i.e., internal nares) found at the back of your mouth to the nasal cavity. After this, the process is similar to that described above.

Inside the nasal cavity, the scent molecules (this time, the flavor molecules that were activated or volatized inside the mouth) bind themselves to olfactory receptors. This triggers a reaction, sending the scent information to the olfactory bulb in your brain. There, the perceived scents are "identified" by matching them with the scents already stored in your scent or olfactory memory.

The Scotch Whisky Research Institute's Flavour Wheel

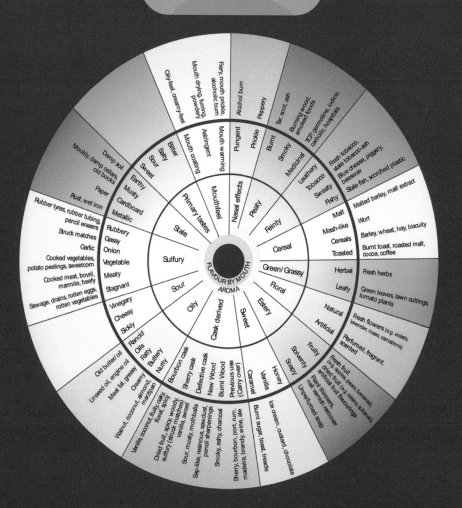

The importance of your scent memory

The above discussion draws attention to the importance of a solid scent memory in tasting Single Malt Scotch Whisky. Without a good scent memory, you will find it difficult to identify the aromas and flavors of Single Malt Scotch Whisky.

As discussed above, in olfaction the aromas and flavors of the whisky detected by your olfactory receptors have to be matched to the scents already stored in your olfactory or scent memory. If your scent memory is lacking, there are a lot of aromas or flavors you will not be able to identify and name.

• Assessing aromas and flavors

Assessing a Single Malt Scotch Whisky's smell is a multi-stage process. For one, you smell it not only through your nose but also through your mouth, as already explained above.

When smelling through the nose, one sniff is not enough to sense all the aromas present in the whisky. As the warmth of your hand is transmitted through the glass to the whisky, the number of detectable aromas should increase, so you should give the whisky time to warm up before you start sniffing it. Some aromas require time to open up, so it is a good idea to sniff the whisky again after it has been sufficiently aerated (i.e., exposed to air). Other aromas will also present themselves only after a bit of water has been added to the whisky, so be sure to sniff the whisky again after water dilution.

When smelling through the mouth, be sure to give the whisky maximum contact with the warmth of your mouth and saliva. By swirling the whisky inside your mouth a few times, you can perceive as many flavors as possible.

When assessing a Single Malt Scotch Whisky's aromas, take note of the complexity of the scents. Are they easy or difficult to identify and describe? Are they multifaceted? Is the whisky open or closed? A closed whisky is one that gives little to no aroma, whereas a whisky that is open has readily detectable aromas. You should also note down every one of the scents or fragrances (aromas and flavors) that you can detect in the whisky, and rate their intensity (e.g., strongly peaty).

• Assessing aftertaste and finish

The sense of smell is also used in assessing a Single Malt Scotch Whisky's aftertaste and finish.

Aftertaste refers to the flavor or flavors (again, these are just scents perceived through the mouth) that linger after you have swallowed the whisky. A pleasant aftertaste that is consistent with the flavors you perceived while the whisky was in your mouth is a mark of a good Single Malt Scotch Whisky.

Finish, on the other hand, refers to the length of time the aftertaste stays or lingers in your mouth. A Single Malt Scotch Whisky can have a short, medium, or long finish. As a general rule, a Single Malt Scotch Whisky with a long or lingering finish is exceptional whisky—provided, of course, that it has a great aftertaste as well.

Touch

What does the whisky "feel" like? Use the tactile senses of your nose and mouth to assess the whisky's nose-feel, mouth-feel, and body.

• Nose-feel

Nose-feel or nasal effects refer to the sensations felt at the back of your nose after you sniff the Single Malt Scotch Whisky. A Single Malt Scotch Whisky's nose-feel is an indicator of its alcoholic strength. A Single Malt Scotch Whisky with a low alcohol content (e.g., 40% ABV) is expected to have less significant nasal effects than a Single Malt Scotch Whisky at cask strength (e.g., 57% ABV).

When sniffing a Single Malt Scotch Whisky, you should be mindful not only of the whisky's scents or aromas but also of the nasal sensation(s) triggered by the whisky. You should answer this question: how did your nose feel when you sniffed the whisky?

The following are the typical nasal effects of a Single Malt Scotch Whisky:

• *Pungent*

This nose-feel is typically associated with high alcoholic strength. Other words that describe a similar nose-feel are burning, biting, and stinging.

- *Prickle*

Use this descriptor if you feel your nose prickling or tingling after sniffing the whisky.

- *Nose-warming*

Use this descriptor if the whisky warmed your nose.

- *Nose-drying*

Use this descriptor if the whisky has a drying effect on your nose.

• Mouth-Feel

Mouth-feel refers to the sensations felt after you sip the Single Malt Scotch Whisky and swirl it inside your mouth. Mouth-feel includes temperature, texture, and body. While it is typically indicative of alcoholic strength, mouth-feel is also usually influenced by the whisky's flavors (the aromas perceived through the mouth).

After sipping the whisky and swirling it a few times in your mouth, answer this question: how did the whisky make your mouth feel? Typical mouth-feel descriptors for Single Malt Scotch Whisky include mouth-warming, astringent, mouth-coating, creamy, and fizzy.

- *Mouth-warming*

Use this if the whisky gives off a sensation of warmth. The higher the whisky's alcoholic strength,

the greater is its expected mouth-warming effect.

- *Astringent*

Use this if the whisky gives rise to a sandpapery feeling in your mouth. This sensation is caused by compounds in the whisky reacting with proteins in your saliva, causing such proteins to clump up or aggregate and the inside of your mouth to feel rough and dry. Basically, whisky that has an astringent mouth-feel has a drying, puckering effect.

- *Mouth-coating*

Use this if the whisky seems to coat the inside of your mouth.

- *Creamy*

Use this if the whisky has a similar texture to or feels like cream inside your mouth.

- *Fizzy*

Use this if the whisky feels effervescent.

Other adjectives used to describe mouth-feel include big, full-bodied (also light-bodied and medium-bodied), thick (viscous), smooth, velvety, oily, soft, and firm.

Taste

What does the whisky taste like? Use your taste buds (the papillae or taste receptors on your tongue) to assess the whisky against the four possible taste values: salty, sweet, sour, and bitter. Again, note that words like spicy, fruity, and smoky are not taste descriptors. They are flavor descriptors and, as explained earlier, they are simply scents perceived through the mouth.

Preparing for the Actual Tasting

A minimum amount of preparation must be done before you begin tasting a Single Malt Scotch Whisky. The following are some of the preparatory steps you can follow:

1. Make sure you are in a room that has ample lighting and minimum sensory distractions.

You will need the light to help you visually assess the whisky. You also do not want to taste whisky in a room that smells strongly of food, cigarettes, air freshener, etc. Such sensory distractions will hinder your ability to accurately identify the whisky's aromas and flavors. By the same logic, you should not wear perfume or use anything that has a distinct or strong odor.

2. Prepare a white background —say a large, white sheet of paper—on your tasting table.

This will help you assess the color of the whisky.

3. Prepare your whisky glass.

Ideally, the glass should be tulip-shaped—that is, it should be wider at the base than at the rim.

The wide, bowl-like base is for swirling the whisky, which you will need to do after you add water so that the water can mix with the whisky. Even if you do not add water to the whisky, you will still need to do some swirling to aerate the whisky. The narrow rim, on the other hand, is necessary to prevent the quick escape of aromas from the glass; the aromas will gather at the rim, giving you time to sniff them properly.

Preferably, the glass should be made of crystal for maximum visual clarity. You should avoid multifaceted drinking glasses that look pretty but distort the physical appearance of the whisky. Patterns or facets on the glass do not matter much if you are blind tasting whisky—but then again, a dark-colored glass is more suited to a blind tasting.

If possible, use glassware that will let you make precise volumetric measurements; look for glassware that has graduated markings on the side. This will help you achieve (and accurately note down) appropriate water-dilution levels later on.

4. Prepare water for dilution.

If you have access to the water used by the distillery in making the whisky, get some of that water and use it.

You can use bottled, distilled water but not mineral water (unless, of course, the mineral water is the same water used in making the whisky). If you want to use tap water, you may, but it must be soft and filtered as you do not want minerals or chlorine. Mineral water and hard water have mineral and salt compounds that could alter the characteristics of the whisky you are evaluating.

Do not use sparkling water as this will obscure the whisky's true texture. You should also refrain from using cold water. Not only could it exaggerate clouding, it could also mask some of the aromas in the whisky.

5. Get a pen and something to write your notes on.

You will need this to note down your observations in the actual tasting.

Step-by-step Guide to Tasting Single Malt Scotch Whisky

Follow these steps when tasting Single Malt Scotch Whisky:

1. Pour about an ounce of the Single Malt Scotch Whisky into your tasting glass.

   Make sure to leave enough room in the glass for dilution with water later on.

2. Tilt the glass at a 45-degree angle toward the white background you have prepared earlier.

   At this point, start visually assessing the whisky's physical characteristics. Assess the whisky's color, viscosity, and clarity. When describing the appearance of the whisky, be as specific as possible.

3. Gently swirl the whisky inside the glass for a few seconds then, holding the glass at eye-level, check out the whisky's "legs" or "tears."

   Legs or tears refer to the "runs" or patterns tracked by

the whisky on the side of the glass as it flows down toward the glass's bottom. The term "legs" or "tears" in the context of a Single Malt Scotch Whisky tasting is the same as the term "legs" or "tears" in the context of a wine tasting.

Tip: The longer the legs (i.e., the longer the streaks left by the whisky on the side of the glass), the more viscous or the thicker the whisky is, and the richer you can expect its texture (mouth-feel) to be. Single Malt Scotch Whiskies with long legs, moreover, typically have high alcoholic strength.

Another tip: If the whisky has long legs or tears, you should be extra careful when it is time to sniff the whisky. Keep it at a distance when you sniff it. An incautious whiff of a strongly alcoholic whisky might hurt your nose and temporarily numb your sense of smell.

4. Cup the whisky glass in your hands then, using one hand, gently swirl the whisky for a few seconds.

Cupping the whisky glass with both hands will warm the whisky in the glass. Swirling, on the other hand, will help aerate the whisky. Both of these steps will help the whisky open up—reveal its aromas.

5. With the whisky glass positioned far from your nose, look down the glass and continue your visual inspection of the whisky.

Is the whisky bright and clear or cloudy and hazy? Can you detect oily or fatty compounds floating on the surface of the whisky?

6. Start raising the glass toward your nose.

It is important that you do this slowly and gradually, so you can stop raising the glass before the alcohol becomes too much for your nose. If you are not careful, the whisky might desensitize your nose and make you unable to complete the next steps (at least for a while).

7. Start sniffing the whisky.

Sniff the aromas that have gathered at the rim of the whisky glass.

i. First, assess the whisky's nose-feel. Is it pungent, prickling, nose-warming, or nose-drying?

ii. Next, assess the whisky's complexity.

iii. Third, assess its openness. Is the whisky open (the aromas are readily detectable) or is it closed (there is little to no aroma present)?

iv. Fourth, identify the whisky's aromas. Is it fruity, peaty, grassy, leafy, or medicinal on the nose? Use The Scotch Whisky Research Institute's Flavour Wheel if you need help in identifying scents.

v. Fifth, rate the aromas according to intensity. Just use a standard scale for rating intensity (e.g., on a scale of 1 to 5).

8. Take a small sip of the whisky.

Do not swallow the whisky just yet. Swirl it around in your mouth. Now, use your sense of touch, sense of taste, and sense of smell.

i. First, assess the whisky's mouth-feel. Is it astringent, mouth-warming, creamy, fizzy, or mouth-coating? Is it heavy and full-bodied? If you want, you can rate the intensity of the whisky's mouth-feel characteristics.

ii. Second, assess the whisky's taste. Is it sweet, salty, bitter, or sour? You can also rate the intensity of the taste.

iii. Third, assess the flavors of the whisky. Is it peaty, smoky, or spicy? Do not forget to assess and rate the flavors' complexity and intensity and the whisky's flavor-openness. Use The Scotch Whisky Research Institute's Flavour Wheel if you need help in identifying scents.

9. Swallow the whisky and assess its aftertaste and finish.

Some prefer spitting out the whisky at this point, but you should really swallow it if you want to feel the full impact of the whisky's finish.

Now assess the aftertaste and finish. Describe the aftertaste and note down the length of time the flavor(s) lingered after you swallowed the whisky.

10. Repeat steps four to nine a few more times.

Feel free to experiment with the number of times you sniff and taste the Single Malt Scotch Whisky.

11. Add water to the whisky in the glass and swirl.

When you are ready for dilution, add water to the whisky and swirl. Since it is difficult to tell the right amount of dilution, start by diluting your whisky with only the smallest amount (a few drops) of water. Be sure to note down the amount of water you added, however, so you can calculate the whisky's post-dilution alcoholic strength.

After dilution, repeat the previous steps to re-evaluate the whisky. You can do this several times, adding more water each time to find out if (and at what point) dilution leads to changes in the whisky's characteristics.

It is ultimately up to you to experiment diluting until you find the optimal tasting experience. The amount of dilution needed will greatly vary depending on the type of glass you use. The more closed the glass rim is, the more dilution you would normally require.

Important Note
Just like an excellent wine, a technically excellent Single Malt Scotch Whisky is one where all the elements work together in perfect balance or harmony. What you see should be what you get when you finally smell, taste, and evaluate the whisky using your senses. For instance, if your visual inspection of the whisky led you to expect a high alcoholic content then you should get a pungent nose-feel when you sniff it, and a full-bodied and mouth-coating mouthfeel when you sip it. Otherwise, something might be wrong with the way you are assessing it.

It must be noted, however, that technical excellence does not necessarily mean superiority – i.e., a technically excellent whisky is not necessarily the best whisky. Whichever Single Malt Scotch Whisky best suits your personal tastes and preferences should be the best Single Malt Scotch Whisky *for you*.

Important Whisky Tasting Tip

If you want to get the most out of your whisky tasting and nosing, you should spend some time training your nose to recognize as many scents or aromas as possible. There are tools you can use to do this such as the *Le Nez du Vin* (Wine Aromas) kits.

Le Nez du Vin can help build your scent vocabulary; many of the aromas found in whisky can be found in this wine aromas kit. For many years now, Wine Aromas has also been requesting that a whisky aromas kit be made, so I'm happy to tell you that *Le Nez du Whisky* is due for release at the end of 2013. You should also keep your eyes open for the release of the WhiskyVibe app, currently in the works. For updates, visit www.WhiskyVibe.com/app.

Most of us have neglected our sense of smell; sometimes, we are even unable to name a scent—however familiar to us it seems to be—until we visually (or in any other sensory way) confirm its source. For instance, the smell of banana may be familiar to us, but we may still be unable to name it (i.e., we are unable to say that the smell is that of banana) until we actually see the banana.

This is lamentable because humans actually have an innately amazing sense of smell. We have around five million olfactory receptors in our nose. Humans are designed to be highly sensitive to scents and odors, but we have gotten nose lazy over time.

To any whisky-tasting enthusiast, this is good news. This means that we are physically equipped to taste and nose whisky. It is just a matter of training and teaching our nose (and our brain) to detect more aromas than it currently can, and building our scent memory and vocabulary, so we can put a name to every scent we smell in our beloved Single Malt Scotch Whisky.

SINGLE MALT SCOTCH WHISKY ETIQUETTE

Is it proper to add ice to Single Malt Scotch Whisky? This section answers this and all other questions related to Single Malt Scotch Whisky etiquette.

Just What Do We Mean by "Etiquette"?

Before we delve deeper into what could very well be a controversial topic, let us first turn our attention to the word "etiquette." By clearly defining our premise, we can properly situate or put into the proper context our upcoming discussion.

According to Merriam-Webster.com, etiquette is *"the conduct or procedure required by good breeding or prescribed by authority to be observed in social or official life."*[1] We cannot use that definition as it is, obviously. There is clearly no one in a position of authority to decree the proper way of enjoying Single Malt Scotch Whisky, and we are not talking about official functions here. So our working definition of etiquette, at this point, is *"the conduct or procedure required by good breeding to be observed in social life."* This is still much too vague a definition, so I am turning to Wikipedia, which defines etiquette as *"a code of behavior that delineates expectations for social behavior according to contemporary conventional norms within a society, social class, or group."*[2]

Now, we can finally define Single Malt Scotch Whisky etiquette. It is *the expected code of conduct when it comes to Single Malt Scotch Whisky, the performance or practice of which indicates good breeding and leads to acceptance.* Since we are particularly concerned with "enjoying" Single Malt Scotch Whisky," we should narrow down our definition further. Thus, we define Single Malt Scotch Whisky etiquette as *the expected way of enjoying and drinking Single Malt Scotch Whisky, the performance or practice of which indicates good breeding and leads to acceptance.*

If you noticed, our definition is somewhat lacking in that it does not specify a social reference—i.e., the social group in which the behavior referred to in our definition is expected and accepted. Here, we cannot help but be a bit arbitrary. We shall limit our definition to the accepted and expected conduct among Single Malt Scotch Whisky connoisseurs and industry professionals.

Thus, for the purposes of the discussion in this chapter, we will take Single Malt Scotch Whisky etiquette to mean *the way of enjoying and drinking Single Malt Scotch Whisky—expected by Single Malt Scotch Whisky connoisseurs and industry professionals—the performance or practice of which indicates good breeding and leads to acceptance in this elite circle of connoisseurs and industry professionals.*

Now that we have covered all the necessary bases, let's proceed to our discussion of Single Malt Scotch Whisky etiquette, starting on the question of whether adding ice to a glass of Single Malt Scotch Whisky is taboo or not.

Drink It with Ice

You hear people in bars say this all the time, "Give me a short Scotch on the rocks." As you already probably know, that's simply Scotch poured over ice.

Now the question is, is it proper to drink a Single Malt Scotch Whisky "on the rocks?"

What is the expected behavior?

Now, let's evaluate this practice of adding ice to Single Malt Scotch Whisky against our working definition of Single Malt Scotch Whisky etiquette, namely, *the way of enjoying and drinking Single Malt Scotch Whisky—expected by Single Malt Scotch Whisky connoisseurs and industry professionals—the performance or practice of which indicates good breeding and leads to acceptance in this elite circle of connoisseurs and industry professionals.*

So, is it accepted behavior to add ice to Single Malt Scotch Whisky? I think the joke below says it all:[3]

Q: What is the fastest way to get stoned?

A: Whisky on the rocks.

Traditionalists would probably love to throw stones at anyone who dares to add ice to their most beloved Single Malt Scotch Whisky.

A quick survey of the literature shows that there is a clear bias against adding ice to Single Malt Scotch Whisky. Let me put it another way, when drinking and enjoying Single Malt Scotch Whisky, NOT adding ice is the behavior expected and accepted by Single Malt Scotch Whisky connoisseurs and industry professionals. So yes, based on our definition of Single Malt Scotch Whisky etiquette, adding ice to Single Malt Scotch Whisky is "an awful waste," "such a shame," and "stupid," to name a few of the more colorful adjectives I have encountered in discussions about ice and Single Malt Scotch Whisky.

There are three main reasons why adding ice is generally considered to be such an insult to Single Malt Scotch Whisky—particularly to a great Single Malt Scotch Whisky:

- First, the cold from the ice can numb your tongue, desensitizing it and rendering you unable to fully appreciate the taste of the Single Malt Scotch Whisky you are drinking.

- Second, ice chills the whisky and this changes the balance of compounds in the whisky. This in turn changes the whisky's organoleptic properties (properties detectable by your senses). In layman's terms, ice changes the aromas and flavors of the Single Malt Scotch Whisky. The general consensus is that the cold from the ice "closes up" the Single Malt Scotch. Thus, the addition of ice will lead to a loss of aromas.

- Third, when the ice melts the whisky's water content increases significantly—and this upsets the balance of the alcohol, water, and flavor compounds in the whisky which, in turn, leads to a change in the whisky's characteristics (particularly its aromas and flavors). Professional tasters often add water to their whisky to volatize some of its trapped aromas; however, the amount of water in ice cubes is enough to drown the whisky.

But then again ...

Now here is my own take. You should do what you want. If you enjoy ice in your Single Malt Scotch Whisky, add ice to your whisky. If you do not like Scotch on the rocks, then do not add ice to your Single Malt Scotch.

If you care about other people's sensibilities—note the word *if*—learn to adjust your behavior depending on the context. If you are with people who could not care less about how you enjoy your Single Malt, you should be able to add as much ice as you want to your whisky. If you are with connoisseurs and professional tasters who are very passionate about the "no ice" rule, you should drink your Scotch neat.

I recommend following just one guideline. If you are drinking Single Malt Scotch Whisky to "taste" it (as a professional whisky taster would), follow the prevailing norm and do not add ice to your whisky.

At this point, it should be noted that there's evidence to suggest that adding ice to a Single Malt Scotch Whisky may actually help open up rather than close up the aromatics of whisky.[4] It is argued that the reduction in temperature promotes the dissolution of alcohol chains in the whisky. When this happens, the flavor compounds trapped within the newly dissolved alcohol molecule chains are released so you get more—not less—aromas when you add ice to your Single Malt Scotch Whisky.

That said, make sure your ice does not smell of anything else. For instance, beware of using old ice which may have absorbed whatever smells are present in your freezer. It is for this reason that I like to use cooling stones when I wish to cool down my Scotch.

So what should it be? Should you or should you not add ice to Single Malt Scotch Whisky during whisky tastings? I suggest that you follow the steps I have outlined in the Tasting Technique section of this chapter, and then if you want to assess the effect of ice on your whisky, make "addition of ice" step #12 of your routine. After that, repeat your evaluation of the whisky's characteristics to determine if adding ice has a significant effect on the whisky.

Drink It "Long"

Drinking Single Malt Scotch Whisky "long" typically means drinking it mixed with other beverages—usually with cola

or soft drinks. Now, is this acceptable based on our definition of Single Malt Scotch Whisky etiquette?

"How dare you?"

This is probably the first reaction of those who passionately love their Single Malt Scotch Whisky. In mixed-up drinks, the Single Malt Scotch Whisky is not even the main attraction—it plays second fiddle to the soft drinks. For those who cannot even countenance the thought of adding ice to their Single Malt Scotch Whisky, turning Single Malt Scotch Whisky into a mixer can only be a grave insult.

Unfortunately, reality bites. The Scotch Whisky industry needs young followers if it is to survive and continue to thrive.[5] If young people do not like their Single Malt Scotch Whisky neat, Scotch Whisky distillers have no choice but to grit their teeth, smile, and tell these young people how wonderful Scotch is mixed with soft drinks.

The verdict

Drinking Single Malt Scotch Whisky "long" is generally not acceptable to industry professionals and connoisseurs. Distillers and their representatives might tell you, "Sure, you will love Scotch long," but that is the businessman talking. Offer them a Scotch mixed with a soft drink, and they probably will not touch it with a ten-foot pole (unless, of course, they are in an event they arranged for the purpose of promoting Scotch Whisky as a mixer).

Even faced with the pressing need to attract young consumers to Single Malt Scotch Whisky, connoisseurs and industry professionals will often draw the line when it comes to actually pushing people to mix Single Malt Scotch Whisky with soft drinks and other types of beverages. Often, they will say something like, "Scotch Whisky is a great mixer, but you should probably leave the mixing to Blended Scotch. As for Single Malt Scotch, it is best to take it neat."

Thus, if you are at a bar and a Single Malt Scotch Whisky connoisseur seated on a stool nearby hears you say this to the bartender, "Give me two fingers of that Lagavulin 16 years and mix it with some Coke®, please," prepare yourself for the derisive look that is sure to come your way.

But then again ...

The decision to drink whisky long is up to you. If you love Single Malt Scotch Whisky with soft drinks, that is your decision. The whisky industry, at least, should thank you. Just remember, though, that there are other much more interesting ways of drinking whisky than mixing it with soft drinks.

For a great whisky mixer, look for a great mixologist. A mixologist is someone who specializes in preparing mixed drinks. He is more than a bartender; he makes his own cocktail creations and designs concoctions based on his study of the craft, his experience mixing drinks, and his knowledge of the ingredients available to him.

In the hands of an expert mixologist, a Single Malt Scotch Whisky cocktail can actually be amazing.

Water It Down

What does water do to whisky anyway? Adding water to whisky activates some of the dormant flavor compounds in the whisky. For this reason, professional tasters often add water to their whisky during whisky tastings. However, they do so only after they have thoroughly evaluated the whisky with no ice or water added.

So what is the etiquette when drinking or enjoying whisky in a non-tasting setting? There's no clear bias for or against adding water to Single Malt Scotch Whisky. You will get a different answer depending on whom you ask. Traditionalists will repeat their worn-out chorus "No ice, no water." Others will probably tell you, it is all right as long as you do the following:

- add only a few drops of water,
- use only cool (not cold) water, and
- if possible, use the same water used by the distillery in making the Single Malt Scotch Whisky (if this is not possible, use distilled [not mineral] water or soft [not hard] tap water).

Give It to Me Neat

Neat Single Malt Scotch Whisky is pure, undiluted whisky. It is whisky with no ice or water added—and *"neat is the*

way of enjoying Single Malt Scotch Whisky, expected by Single Malt Scotch Whisky connoisseurs and industry professionals, the performance or practice of which indicates good breeding and leads to acceptance in this elite circle of connoisseurs and industry professionals."

There really is no question. This is the widely accepted way of enjoying Single Malt Scotch Whisky. Traditionalists insist on this; those who do not like their Single Malt Scotch neat still accept it even if they do not practice it.

Glassware

What is the right type of glassware for drinking Single Malt Scotch Whisky? The answer depends on the context.

Drinking for enjoyment

There really is no right type of glassware for enjoying Single Malt Scotch Whisky. Some people may insist that you use only a particular type of glassware, but unless you are in a Single Malt Scotch Whisky tasting, use any type of glassware you want.

If in a tasting

I believe we have already covered the basics of Single Malt Scotch Whisky glassware in our discussion of tasting techniques. However, let's reiterate the most salient points here.

First, you want a glass that is shaped like a tulip: wide at the base and narrow at the rim. The wide base will give you room in which to swirl your whisky. The narrow rim will catch the aromas escaping from the whisky, making it easier for you to assess them properly.

Second, you want a glass that is made of crystal. Crystal is best for assessing the appearance of the Single Malt Scotch Whisky. Do not use cut-crystal, colored-crystal or multifaceted crystal glasses since these types of glassware will not give you a clear view of the Single Malt Scotch in your glass.

In a Single Malt Scotch Whisky tasting, you are also advised to use a glass with graduated markings.

Types of glassware

The following are the usual types of Scotch Whisky glassware:

- *Tulip-shaped snifters*
  This is a short-stemmed glass with a wide bowl-like base tapering up to a narrow rim. The snifter is the preferred glassware type for nosing Single Malt Scotch Whisky.

- *Traditional whisky tumblers*
  The typical whisky tumbler is a short, stout glass without a stem. It can be wider at the rim than at the base, or the rim and the base can be the same size.

- *Elongated whisky tumblers*
  Like the traditional whisky tumbler, it does not have a stem and sits on a heavy, round base. However, it is taller than the traditional whisky tumbler. It is also wider at the base than at the rim; the rim may or may not have a slight flare.

- *Thistle-shaped whisky glass*
  This type of whisky glass looks like a combination of the elongated whisky tumbler and the snifter. It is a stemmed glass, like the snifter, but its stem is shorter, so it sits much lower on the ground than the snifter. Like the elongated whisky tumbler, the thistle-shaped whisky glass has elongated sides which may or may not end in a flare at the rim.

- *Glencairn Glass*

  This looks like an elongated, tulip-shaped snifter. Unlike a snifter, it does not have a narrow stem. It sits on a stout "foot" instead. Like a snifter, it has a wide, bowl-like base and a narrow rim. It has elongated sides and looks taller than the typical snifter.

- *BV Whisky Tot Glass*

  The Bottega del Vino Johnson's Whisky Tot looks like an elongated, tulip-shaped snifter. The stemless, semi-wide, bowl-like base tapers up to a slight constriction just below the flared lip. This is a great glass for sipping whisky, and it is my personal favorite. *See glass on page 62.*

- *NEAT™ Glass*

  The NEAT™ glass (NEAT™ stands for Naturally Engineered Aroma Technology) looks like a short, flattened, tulip-shaped snifter. The wide bowl facilitates swirling, the constricted neck concentrates aromas, and the flared rim allows ethanol to escape, minimizing nose burn and revealing masked aromas.

Cooling Stones

Let's say you like your whisky cool, but you do want to conform to Single Malt Scotch Whisky etiquette of not adding ice to your dram. In that case, can you use cooling stones instead?

What are cooling stones?

These are small, square cubes or cylindrical disks crafted out of soapstone. When you first get them, wash them thoroughly with water, dry them completely, and then put them inside a muslin bag. Next, store them in the freezer for a few days. When they are ready, put one of the disks or a few of the cubes inside your whisky glass and pour whisky over them.

The cooling stones will give your whisky a little chill. Unlike ice, they will not melt and water down your Single Malt Scotch.

BV - Equinox -Double Old Fashioned with cooling stones (Tumbler style glass)

Should you or should you not?

Using cooling stones is a much better option than using ice cubes. They will keep your whisky cool without chilling it excessively, so the cold will not numb your senses and should not lessen the aromas of your whisky. They will not melt, so they will not drown your Scotch. Finally, soapstone does not react with or absorb whisky; they are also soft and slippery and will not scratch your prized crystal glassware.

All in all, cooling stones will make your Single Malt Scotch Whisky cooler than usual, but not so cold that your senses will go numb. And if—again, note the word *if*—the tale, I have read about the origin of the phrase "Scotch on the rocks" is true, then using cooling stones should be okay. According to this tale, Scots used stones cooled in streams to cool their whisky—thus the term Scotch on the rocks.[6] If this is true, using cooling stones to cool your Single Malt would be doing exactly what the Scots did before there were refrigerators and ice cubes.

Endnotes

1 Etiquette. (n.d.). Merriam-Webster. Date accessed: July 18, 2011 (http://www.merriam-webster.com/dictionary/etiquette).

2 Etiquette. (July 17, 2011). *In Wikipedia, The Free Encyclopedia*. Date accessed: July 18, 2011 (http://en.wikipedia.org/w/index.php?title=Etiquette&oldid=439880446).

3 Alternative Whisky Academy. (n.d.). Whisky jokes and whisky quotes. Date accessed: July 18 (http://www.awa.dk/whisky-/jokes/index.htm).

4 Lersch, Martin. (June 3, 2007). New perspectives on whisky and water. Date accessed: July 18, 20011 (http://blog.khymos.org/2007/06/03/new-perspectives-on-whisky-and-water/).

5 Ipsen, Erik. (May 21, 1994). After 500 years, Scotch finally decides it can mix. Date accessed: July 18, 2011 (http://www.nytimes.com/1994/05/21/business/worldbusiness/21iht-scotch.html).

6 Kimou. (July 15, 2011). Whisky. In *The UK Plumbing Forum*. Date accessed: July 18, 2011 (http://www.ukplumbersforums.co.uk/general-off-topic-chat/23038-whisky.html).

•Chapter V•

Styles of Single Malt Scotch Whisky

How do you classify Single Malt Scotch Whiskies? The answer to this question is explored in great detail in this chapter.

Single Malt Scotch Whiskies are classified in three ways—i.e., by *cluster*, by *region,* and by *type*—and these classification systems can help you in your Single Malt Scotch selections.

Single malt classification systems (especially the cluster system) simplify the task of choosing whiskies. If you like a particular Single Malt Scotch and you know this single malt's type, region, and cluster, you can make an educated guess about which other single malts you would like; you can simply look for another Single Malt Scotch that is of the same type, region, and/or cluster as the Single Malt Scotch you like.

"I love this Laphroaig 12 yrs. Now what other Single Malt Scotch Whiskies might I like?

I see that the Caol Ila 12 yrs is from an Islay distiller (region classification system: match), belongs to Cluster J (Wishart's cluster classification system: match) and is 12 years old, too (type classification system: match).

Therefore, I might enjoy the Caol Ila 12 yrs just as much as I enjoy the Laphroaig 12 yrs.

THE SINGLE MALT SCOTCH WHISKY CLUSTERS

The cluster classification system is based on flavor or, to be more precise, on single malt characteristics. What a cluster classification system does is categorize single malts according to their predominant features such as aroma, flavor, mouth-feel, and finish.

In this book, we'll focus on three cluster classification systems:

- the 10-cluster system developed by David Wishart,
- the 12-cluster system developed by LaPointe and Legendre, and
- the flavour map developed by Broom and Beveridge.

David Wishart's Cluster Classification[1]

Using tasting notes in books on malt whisky as well as whatever tasting notes were available from distilleries, David Wishart compiled a list of Single Malt Scotch's taste and aromatic descriptors, which he classified into the following sensory variables:

1. Body (Light - Heavy)
2. Sweetness (Dry - Sweet)
3. Smoky (Peaty)
4. Medicinal (Salty)
5. Feinty (Sulphury)
6. Honey (Vanilla)
7. Spicy (Woody)
8. Winey (Sherry)
9. Nutty (Oaky to Creamy)
10. Malty (Cerealy)
11. Fruity (Estery)
12. Floral (Herbal)

Wishart then chose 86 single malts, ranging in age from 10 to 15 years, and assessed their taste and aromatic characteristics. Once all 86 single malts had been properly described and analyzed, clustering software was used to create groups or clusters of single malts that have matching characteristics across the above-listed 12 variables.

Wishart's 10 clusters

Wishart's cluster analysis yielded 10 single malt clusters.

• Cluster A

Characteristics: Full-Bodied, Medium-Sweet, Pronounced Sherry with Fruity, Spicy, Malty Notes and Nutty, Smoky Hints

Single Malts: Balmenach, Dailuaine, Dalmore, Glendronach, Macallan, Mortlach, Royal Lochnagar

• Cluster B

Characteristics: Medium-Bodied, Medium-Sweet, with Nutty, Malty, Floral, Honey and Fruity Notes

Single Malts: Aberfeldy, Aberlour, Ben Nevis, Benrinnes, Benromach, Blair Athol, Cragganmore, Edradour, Glenfarclas, Glenturret, Knockando, Longmorn, Scapa, Strathisla

• Cluster C

Characteristics: Medium-Bodied, Medium-Sweet, with Fruity, Floral, Honey, Malty Notes and Spicy Hints

Single Malts: Balvenie, Benriach, Dalwhinnie, Glendullan, Glen Elgin, Glenlivet, Glen Ord, Linkwood, Royal Brackla

• Cluster D

Characteristics: Light, Medium-Sweet, Low or No Peat, with Fruity, Floral, Malty Notes and Nutty Hints

Single Malts: An Cnoc, Auchentoshan, Aultmore, Cardhu, Glengoyne, Glen Grant, Mannochmore, Speyside, Tamdhu, Tobermory

• Cluster E

Characteristics: Light, Medium-Sweet, Low Peat, with Floral, Malty Notes and Fruity, Spicy, Honey Hints

Single Malts: Bladnoch, Bunnahabhain, Glenallachie, Glenkinchie, Glenlossie, Glen Moray, Inchgower, Inchmurrin, Tomintoul

• Cluster F

Characteristics: Medium-Bodied, Medium-Sweet, Low Peat, Malty Notes and Sherry, Honey, Spicy Hints

Single Malts: Ardmore, Auchroisk, Deanston, Glen Deveron, Glen Keith, Glenrothes, Old Fettercairn, Tomatin, Tormore, Tullibardine

• Cluster G

Characteristics: Medium-Bodied, Sweet, Low Peat and Floral Notes

Single Malts: Arran, Dufftown, Glenfiddich, Glen Spey, Miltonduff, Speyburn

• Cluster H

Characteristics: Medium-Bodied, Medium-Sweet, with Smoky, Fruity, Spicy Notes and Floral, Nutty Hints

Single Malts: Balblair, Craigellachie, Glen Garioch, Glenmorangie, Oban, Old Pulteney, Strathmill, Tamnavulin, Teaninich

• Cluster I

Characteristics: Medium-Light, Dry, with Smoky, Spicy, Honey Notes and Nutty, Floral Hints

Single Malts: Bowmore, Bruichladdich, Glen Scotia, Highland Park, Isle of Jura, Springbank

• Cluster J

Characteristics: Full-Bodied, Dry, Pungent, Peaty and Medicinal, with Spicy, Feinty Notes

Single Malts: Ardbeg, Caol Ila, Clynelish, Lagavulin, Laphroaig, Talisker

LaPointe and Legendre's Cluster Classification[2]

LaPointe and Legendre's cluster classification system groups Single Malt Scotch Whiskies according to their color, body, nose, palate, and finish. To develop their clusters, they scored 109 Single Malt Scotch Whiskies across a total of 68 Scotch characteristics:

(a) Color
white wine, yellow, very pale, pale, pale gold, gold, old gold, full gold, bronze, pale amber, amber, full amber, red, fino sherry

(b) Nose
aromatic, peaty, sweet, light, fresh, dry, fruity, grassy, salty, sherry, spicy, rich

(c) Body
soft, medium, full, round, smooth, light, firm, oily

(d)Palate
full, dry, sherry, big, light, smooth, clean, fruity, grassy, smoky, sweet, spicy, oily, salty, aromatic

(e) Finish
full, dry, warm, big, light, smooth, clean, fruity, grassy, smoky, sweet, spicy, oily, salty, aromatic, quick, long, very long, lingering

LaPointe and Legendre used Ward's (1963) minimum vari-

ance clustering method to create their Single Malt Scotch
Whisky clusters. This procedure yielded 12 clusters or
groups.

LaPointe and Legendre's 12 clusters

The following are the 12 single
malt whisky clusters in LaPointe
and Legendre's cluster classification system:

• Group A

Average characteristics:

Color	Nose	Body	Palate	Finish
full gold	fruity, salty	medium	oily, salty, sherry	dry

Single Malts: Aberfeldy, Glenugie, Laphroaig, Scapa

• Group B

Average characteristics:

Color	Nose	Body	Palate	Finish
amber	sweet, sherry	medium, smooth	dry, sweet	long

Single Malts: Aberlour, Balvenie,
Benrinnes, Dalmore, Glendul-
lan, Glenlivet, Glenturret, High-
land Park, Lochside, Macallan,
Millburn, Oban, Singleton of
Auchroisk, Strathisla

• Group C

Average characteristics:

Color	Nose	Body	Palate	Finish
pale gold	sweet, salty	medium to full, oily	sweet, spicy	big, long, spicy

Single Malts: Ardmore, Blair
Athol, Clynelish, Glenmorangie, Port Ellen, Talisker

• Group D

Average characteristics:

Color	Nose	Body	Palate	Finish
pale gold	fruity, grassy	oily	sweet, fruity	sweet, quick

Single Malts: Auchentoshan,
Ben Nevis, Coleburn, Speyburn

• Group E

Average characteristics:

Color	Nose	Body	Palate	Finish
pale wyne, gold	fruity, peaty	light	sweet, spicy	fruity

Single Malts: Balblair, Bladnoch,
Caol Ila, Edradour, Glenburgie,
Inchmurrin, Inverleven, Kin-
claith, Littlemill, Pulteney

• Group F

Average characteristics:

Color	Nose	Body	Palate	Finish
gold	aromatic	medium, smooth, light	sweet	sweet

Single Malts: Aultmore, Benriach, Benromach, Bunnahabhain, Cardhu, Dalwhinnie, Glenallachie, Glen Deveron, Glenkinchie, Glen Scotia, Inchgower, Knockando, Miltonduff, Springbank, Tullibardine

• Group G

Average characteristics:

Color	Nose	Body	Palate	Finish
gold, full gold	grassy	smooth, light	grassy	dry

Single Malts: Cragganmore, Glenglassaugh, Glen Moray, Longmorn, Rosebank, Tamnavulin, Tomintoul

• Group H

Average characteristics:

Color	Nose	Body	Palate	Finish
white wyne, pale	sweet	smooth, light	sweet, dry, fruity, smoky	dry, light

Single Malts: Bruichladdich, Deanston, Fettercairn, Glenfiddich, Glen Mhor, Glen Spey, Glentauchers, Ladyburn, Tobermory

• Group I

Average characteristics:

Color	Nose	Body	Palate	Finish
gold, full gold, bronze	dry, peaty	medium, light, firm	dry, smoky, sweet	salty

Single Malts: Ardbeg, Bowmore, Dufftown, Glenfarclas, Glenlochy, Glenury Royal, Jura, Lagavulin, Longrow (Springbank distillery)

• Group J

Average characteristics:

Color	Nose	Body	Palate	Finish
full gold	dry, peaty, sherry	light to medium, round	sweet	dry

Single Malts: Glen Albyn, Glengoyne, Glen Grant, Glenlossie, Linkwood, North Port, Saint Magdalene, Tamdhu

• Group K

Average characteristics:

Color	Nose	Body	Palate	Finish
gold, full gold	sweet, dry, peaty	medium to full	sweet, dry	dry, long

Single Malts: Balmenach, Brackla, Convalmore, Craigellachie, Dailuaine, Dallas Dhu, Glendronach, Glenesk, Glen Keith, Glenordie (Glen Ord), Glenrothes, Knockdhu, Mortlach, Tomatin, Tormore

• Group L

Average characteristics:

Color	Nose	Body	Palate	Finish
full gold	aromatic, peaty	medium	sweet, smoky	smoky

Single Malts: Banff, Caper-donich, Glencadam, Glen Elgin, Glen Garioch, Imperial, Loch-nagar, Teaninich

The Single Malt Flavor Map[3]

The Single Malt Whisky Flavour Map, developed by Dave Broom and Jim Beveridge, provides a simple and intuitive way of classifying single malt whiskies according to their flavor profile.

The flavor map's features

This cluster classification system plots single malts on a flavor grid. The grid is composed of two axes that divide the plane into four quadrants: the *Smoky and Rich* quadrant, the *Rich and Delicate* quadrant, the *Delicate and Light* quadrant, and the *Light and Smoky* quadrant. On these quadrants are plotted the 22 single malts that Broom and Beveridge have already rated based on how light/rich and how delicate/ smoky they are.

However, the flavor map does more than just tell you whether a single malt whisky is Smoky and Rich, Rich and Delicate, Delicate and Light, or Light and Smoky. If you look at the map on the next page, you will see that the whiskies tend to form clusters or groups.

There are four main single malt whisky clusters in the map (they are color-coded for convenience), and each cluster represents a unique flavor profile.

• Light and Floral

This cluster is characterized by fresh, floral, and grassy flavors. Four of the twenty-two whiskies on the map have this flavor profile:

- Knockando 12 Yr Old
- Glenfiddich 12 Yr Old
- Glenlivet 12 Yr Old
- Glenkinchie 12 Yr Old

• Fruity and Spicy

This cluster overlaps all quadrants, but tends to gravitate toward the Delicate and Light

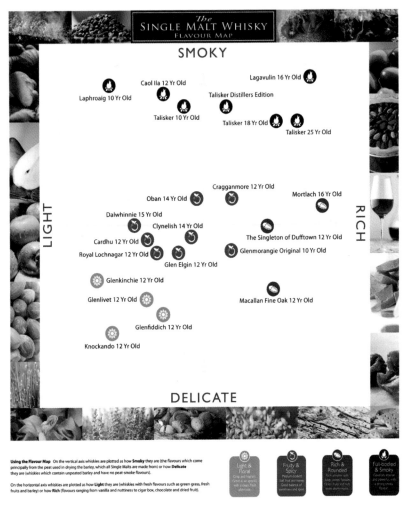

The Single Malt Whisky
SINGLE MALT WHISKY
FLAVOUR MAP

SMOKY

Lagavulin 16 Yr Old

Caol Ila 12 Yr Old

Laphroaig 10 Yr Old

Talisker Distillers Edition

Talisker 10 Yr Old

Talisker 18 Yr Old   Talisker 25 Yr Old

LIGHT

Cragganmore 12 Yr Old

Oban 14 Yr Old

Mortlach 16 Yr Old

Dalwhinnie 15 Yr Old

Clynelish 14 Yr Old

The Singleton of Dufftown 12 Yr Old

Cardhu 12 Yr Old

Royal Lochnagar 12 Yr Old

Glenmorangie Original 10 Yr Old

Glen Elgin 12 Yr Old

RICH

Glenkinchie 12 Yr Old

Glenlivet 12 Yr Old

Macallan Fine Oak 12 Yr Old

Glenfiddich 12 Yr Old

Knockando 12 Yr Old

DELICATE

Using the Flavour Map   On the vertical axis whiskies are plotted as how **Smoky** they are (the flavours which come principally from the peat used in drying the barley, which all Single Malts are made from) or how **Delicate** they are (whiskies which contain unpeated barley and have no peat-smoke flavours).

On the horizontal axis whiskies are plotted as how **Light** they are (whiskies with fresh flavours such as green grass, fresh fruits and barley) or how **Rich** (flavours ranging from vanilla and nuttiness to cigar box, chocolate and dried fruit).

Light & Floral
Crisp and marshy. Great as an aperitif, with a clean, fresh aftertaste.

Fruity & Spicy
Medium-bodied. Soft fruit and honey. Good balance of sweetness and spice.

Rich & Rounded
Rich whiskies with deep, sweet flavours. Dried fruity and nuts, with sherry notes.

Full-bodied & Smoky
Generally intense and powerful, with a strong smoky flavour.

quadrant. As the cluster's name suggests, whiskies that belong to this cluster are fruity and spicy; in general, they have richer flavors than the single malts in the light and floral cluster.

There are 8 single malts in this cluster.

- Royal Lochnagar 12 Yr Old
- Glen Elgin 12 Yr Old
- Glenmorangie Original 10 Yr Old
- Cardhu 12 Yr Old
- Clynelish 14 Yr Old
- Dalwhinnie 15 Yr Old
- Cragganmore 12 Yr Old
- Oban 14 Yr Old

• Rich and Rounded

The flavors of single malts in this cluster exhibit a large oak influence: vanilla, chocolate, nuts, and dried fruits. When it comes to the degree of smokiness, the single malts in this cluster tend to be delicate with little to no peat.

Three of the twenty-two single malts on the flavor map belong to this cluster. They are as follows:

- Macallan Fine Oak 12 Yr Old
- Mortlach 16 Yr Old
- The Singleton of Dufftown 12 Yr Old

• Full Bodied & Smoky

Seven of the twenty-two single malts belong to this cluster and are distributed across the two Smoky quadrants (Smoky and Rich, Light and Smoky).

The whiskies in this cluster are characterized by peatiness and tend to become more complex the higher they go up the Delicate-Smoky axis. Depending on their placement along the Light-Rich axis, the smoky/peaty whiskies in this cluster can be fresh, floral, and grassy, or they can exhibit the flavors of vanilla, nuts, and chocolate.

- Laphroaig 10 Yr Old
- Caol Ila 12 Yr Old
- Talisker 10 Yr Old
- Talisker Distillers Edition
- Talisker 18 Yr Old
- Talisker 25 Yr Old
- Lagavulin 16 Yr Old

How to use this flavor map

In the simplest of uses, the flavor map can be used as a visual reference. It tells you what a particular single malt whisky "tastes" like. If you are up to it, you can also easily build on the map and make it as extensive and as personalized as you want.

You can use the whisky flavor map as a handy guide to choosing a single malt whisky. All you need to do, basically, is to decide on your preferred flavor cluster (you may even consider flavor quadrant placement), and then choose a whisky from that cluster (and quadrant if you are also using this as a reference).

Even if you do not quite know which flavor profile and flavor quadrant you prefer, it does not much matter. Look for a single malt whisky that you know you like; chances are high that you will also like the whiskies that belong to the same cluster as (or are placed close to) that whisky.

The flavor map's usefulness, however, goes beyond the above suggested applications. Note that you can actually expand and make this flavor map your own. Whenever you try a new whisky, you can rate it according to how delicate/smoky and how light/rich it is, and then plot it accordingly on the flavor map. If you know or have tasted some of the 22 already mapped single malts, use them as a reference when plotting the new whisky on the map.

Indeed, the great thing about the flavor map is its flexibility, which allows for subjective classifications. This is rather brilliant because, after all, the ultimate goal of clustering

whiskies is to make it easier for whisky lovers to find and choose whiskies they will like.

THE SINGLE MALT SCOTCH WHISKY REGIONS

In Scotland, there are three protected whisky regions (Highland, Lowland, and Speyside) and two protected whisky localities (Islay and Campbeltown). These protected regions and localities are clearly identified and delineated in the Scotch Whisky Regulations of 2009.

Note: Most people do not make a distinction between "protected whisky regions" and "protected whisky localities." These five protected geographical areas are usually lumped together and collectively referred to as "protected whisky regions," "protected whisky production regions," or "whisky regions."

Apart from the five official whisky regions and whisky localities earlier mentioned, there is one other *de-facto* whisky region in Scotland. This is the Islands. Officially, the Islands Region is part of the Highland Whisky Region.

Scotch whisky enthusiasts, however, generally recognize the Islands as a separate whisky region.

The Three Protected Whisky Regions

The three protected whisky regions are the Highland, the Lowland, and Speyside.

Highland

This is the largest protected whisky region in Scotland. It is found in Northern Scotland and located north of the Lowland Whisky Region, from which it is separated by an imaginary Highland Line.

Note: Under Section 7 of Regulation 10 of the Scotch Whisky Regulations of 2009, the "line dividing the Highland Region from the Lowland Region" is defined as follows:

"… the line beginning at the North Channel and running along the southern foreshore of the Firth of Clyde to Greenock, and from there to Cardross Station, then eastwards in a straight line to the summit of Earl's Seat in the Campsie Fells, and then eastwards in a straight line to the Wallace Monument, and from there eastwards along the line of the B998 and A91 roads until the A91 meets the M90 road at Milnathort, and then along the M90 northwards until the Bridge of Earn, and then along the River Earn until its confluence with the River Tay, and then along the southern foreshore of that river and the Firth of Tay until it comes to the North Sea."[4]

The Highland Region has four major subdivisions: Northern Highlands, Western Highlands, Midlands/Central Highlands, and Eastern Highlands. The Scotch Whisky Association lists 35 Highland Single Malt Scotch Whisky distilleries.[5] As of this writing (and omitting the distilleries classified under Speyside and the unofficial Islands region), however, I count 24 active Highland single malt distilleries.

Unfortunately for those who want an easy way of choosing a single malt whisky, the Highland Region does not lend itself very well to flavor/taste generalizations. The large area covered by this region means that single malt producers have to contend with greatly varying

THE 24 HIGHLAND SINGLE MALT SCOTCH WHISKY DISTILLERIES		
Aberfeldy	Edradour	Loch Lomond
Balblair	(Old) Fettercairn	(Royal) Lochnagar
Ben Nevis	Glen Garioch	Oban
Blair Athol	Glen Ord (Singleton)	Pulteney
Clynelish	Glencadam	Royal Brackla
Dalmore	Glengoyne	Teaninich
Dalwhinnie	Glenmorangie	Tomatin
Deanston	Glenturret	Tullibardine

microclimates, water sources, air quality, and other geographically related factors. These differences, in turn, lead to great variance in the characteristics of Highland single malts.

Cross-referencing the Highland single malts with Wishart's and LaPointe and Legendre's cluster classification systems underscores the great variation among this region's Single Malt Scotch Whiskies. Highland single malts are spread across all clusters except Cluster E and G under Wishart's cluster classification system, while they are spread across all groups with no exceptions under LaPointe and Legendre's cluster classification system.

Lowland

The Lowland Scotch Whisky Region refers to the area that lies between the imaginary Highland Line and the English border. It is the second largest whisky-producing region in Scotland.

The Lowland Region has great soil, a wonderful climate, and plenty of fresh-water sources. By all indications, this region is destined for whisky-production greatness. Unfortunately, the rising popularity of Scotch from the northern part of Scotland has resulted in the Lowland malts' gradual loss of favor through the years. In fact, according to the Scotch Whisky Association's map of distilleries,[6] only four Lowland single malt distilleries remain open today. As of this writing, though, I count 6 Single Malt Scotch distilleries in the Lowland Region.

THE 6 SINGLE MALT WHISKY DISTILLERIES IN THE LOWLAND REGION
Ailsa Bay
Annandale
Auchentoshan
Bladnoch
Daftmill
Glenkinchie

On the upside, Lowland malts are much easier to classify than Highland malts because of the former's generally consistent characteristics (the much smaller number of distilleries probably helps as well). To you this means that if you like one Lowland Single Malt Scotch, chances are high that you will also like other Lowland single malts.

Lowland Single Malt Scotch Whiskies are generally pale golden, light-bodied, sweet, and fruity with low to no peat. They are, in the whole, milder than Highland Single Malt Scotch Whiskies. This makes them less appealing to those who have come to associate Single Malt Scotch with heavy smokiness or peatiness.

Speyside

Speyside is a relatively small piece of land off the northern coast of Scotland. It is bounded on all sides (except the seaward side) by the Highland Region; so while it is officially recognized as a distinct whisky region, it is still practically considered part of the larger Highland Whisky Region. In fact, Speyside distilleries can choose which geographical region to use on their labels. In their single malt bottlings, for instance, they can use either "Speyside Single Malt Scotch Whisky" or "Highland Single Malt Scotch Whisky."

The Speyside Whisky Region is composed of a number of wards:[7]

i. the wards of Buckie, Elgin City North, Elgin City South, Fochabers Lhanbryde, Forres, Heldon and Laich, Keith and Cullen and Speyside Glenlivet of the Moray Council as those wards are constituted in the Moray (Electoral Arrangements) Order 2006(2); and

ii. the Badenoch and Strathspey ward of the Highland Council as that ward is constituted in the Highland (Electoral Arrangements) Order 2006(3).

Speyside is positively miniscule beside the sprawling Highland writing, however, I count 51 malt distilleries in Speyside. The great number of distilleries in the Speyside region means a wide variation of techniques in

THE 51 SINGLE MALT SCOTCH WHISKY DISTILLERIES IN SPEYSIDE		
Aberlour	Glen Grant	Knockdhu
Allt A'Bhainne	Glen Moray	Linkwood
Ardmore	Glen Spey	Longmorn
Auchroisk	Glenallachie	Macallan
Aultmore	Glenburgie	Macduff
Balmenach	Glendronach	Mannochmore
Balvenie	Glendullan	Miltonduff
Benriach	Glenfarclas	Mortlach
Benrinnes	Glenfiddich	Roseisle
Benromach	Glenglassaugh	Speyburn
Braeval	Glenlivet	Speyside
Cardhu	Glenlossie	Strathisla
Cragganmore	Glenrothes	Strathmill
Craigellachie	Glentauchers	Tamdhu
Dailuaine	Inchgower	Tamnavulin
Dufftown	Kininvie	Tomintoul
Glen Elgin	Knockando	Tormore

Region, but it actually has more distilleries than the latter.

According to the Scotch Whisky Association's records, there are 49 Single Malt Scotch Whisky distilleries in Speyside.[8] As of this Scotch Whisky production. Naturally, this translates to differences in the characteristics of Speyside single malts. Nevertheless, since Speyside is a fairly limited region, at least geographically, Speyside single malts exhibit more similarities across the board than do Highland single malts.

Speyside single malts are usually golden in color, ranging from pale gold to full gold. They are predominantly aromatic, sweet, dry, and/or peaty on the nose. Common aroma and flavor descriptors include floral and malty with hints of fruit, spice, nuts, and honey. They are smooth and medium- to full-bodied and, on the palate, they are generally sweet or dry with a long, sweet, or dry finish.

The Two Protected Whisky Localities

The two protected whisky localities are Islay and Campbeltown.

Islay

The protected whisky locality of Islay refers to the Isle of Islay. Located southwest of the Isle of Jura and northwest of Campbeltown, Islay is one of the islands that make up the Southern Hebrides group of islands, and it is administered by the Argyll and Bute Council.

According to the Scotch Whisky Association, the following are the Single Malt Scotch Whisky distilleries in the Islay Region:[9]

THE 8 SINGLE MALT SCOTCH DISTILLERIES IN ISLAY
Ardbeg
Bowmore
Bruichladdich
Bunnahabhain
Caol Ila
Kilchoman
Lagavulin
Laphroaig

The Islay single malts' characteristically strong and rich flavor is due in large part to the geographical characteristics of the Isle of Islay. Since Islay is rich in peat sources, seven of the eight distilleries in this region use peat when drying their malt. It is no wonder then that Islay whiskies have gained a reputation for being intensely peaty and smoky.

That being said, the levels of peatiness and the flavor profiles of Islay single malts are far from uniform. According to Wishart's cluster classification system, the single malts of Ardbeg, Lagavulin, Laphroaig, and Caol Ila are "full-bodied, dry, pungent, peaty, and medicinal, with spicy, feinty notes." Kilchoman, although not classified in Wishart's cluster system, is like a Lagavulin or a Laphroaig in its intensity. Bowmore's and Bruichladdich's single malts are "medium-light, dry, with smoky, spicy, honey notes and nutty, floral hints." Bunnahabhain is the only Islay single malt that is not smoky or peaty, which is understandable since this distillery does not use peated malt. According to Wishart's classification, Bunnahabhain single malts are "light, medium-sweet, low peat, with floral, malty notes and fruity, spicy, honey hints."

Campbeltown

The protected whisky locality of Campbeltown, known for single malts with briny notes, refers to the South Kintyre ward of the Argyll and Bute Council. At one time, there were more than 30 distilleries in this area. Now, only three distilleries remain according to the Scotch Whisky Association.[10]

THE 3 SINGLE MALT DISTILLERIES IN CAMPBELTOWN
Springbank
Glen Scotia
Glengyle Distillery (Kilkerran)

Springbank, Campbeltown's most active and most successful distillery, produces three single malts: Springbank, Longrow, and Hazelburn, each of which exhibits a different set of characteristics. Springbank —a rich and complex Single Malt Scotch with smooth, smoky undertones—is made with lightly peated barley distilled 2.5 times. Longrow—a big-bodied, intensely smoky single malt—is made through double distillation using heavily peated barley. Hazelburn— a light, delicate, and subtly flavored single malt whisky—is Springbank Distillery's cleanest tasting Single Malt Scotch; it is a product of triple distillation using unpeated barley.

Glen Scotia has a very low production volume, but it remains in production mode. Glen Scotia Single Malt is generally described as salty, smoky, and spicy.

Glengyle was reopened in 2004 and is set to release its first 12-year-old bottlings around 2016. Glengyle Distillery's whisky is called Kilkerran Single Malt Scotch Whisky.

The Unofficial Whisky Region

The Islands, which are officially part of the Highland Whisky Region, are not a protected whisky region as per the terms of the Scotch Whisky Regulations of 2009.

Islands

The Islands are a collection of islands (no surprise there) scattered west and north of the Highland Mainland.

Single Malt Scotch whiskies from the Islands typically have salty or briny notes due to the Islands distilleries' coastal location. Island single malts are also generally peaty and smoky due to the Island distilleries' use of peated malt in whisky production.

Seven islands make up the Islands Whisky Region.

The following are the eight Island distilleries; officially, they are part of the Highland Whisky Region:

- **Highland Park** – Located in the Orkney Islands, Highland Park is undeniably one of the world's best-known makers of Single Malt Scotch Whisky. Highland Park Single Malts are distinctively smoky and peaty without being overly intense or heavy.
- **Scapa** – This distillery also operates from Orkney.
- **Abhainn Dearg** – This is a relatively new distillery on the Isle of Lewis.
- **Talisker** – A big name in the world of Single Malt Scotch Whiskies, this distillery is located on the Isle of Skye. It is known for making intensely peaty and smoky single malts.
- **Tobermory** – Located on the Isle of Mull, the Tobermory distillery makes two types of non-chill-filtered single malts: Tobermory and Ledaig. The Tobermory Single Malt Scotch Whisky

THE 7 ISLANDS OF THE ISLANDS REGION		
Orkney Islands	Isle of Skye	Isle of Arran
Isle of Lewis and Harris	Isle of Mull	Isle of Jura
Isle of Barra		

(available in 10-year-old and 15-year-old bottlings) is typically smooth and fruity with a spicy finish. The Ledaig Single Malt Scotch Whisky, on the other hand, has a distinct peat influence because it is made using exclusively peat-dried malt.

- **Isle of Jura** – This distillery is based on Jura.
- **Isle of Arran** – This distillery is based on Arran.
- **Isle of Barra** – This distillery in Barra is not yet producing whisky.

THE SINGLE MALT SCOTCH WHISKY TYPES

There are several types of Single Malt Scotch Whiskies. Variations in types are a result of different production methods.

Single Cask Single Malt Scotch

Also known as Single-Single Malt Scotch Whisky, this is a bottling of a Single Malt Scotch Whisky from a single cask.

Typically, a distillery's Single Malt Scotch Whisky bottling is a blend of single malts from two or more casks. This blending or marriage between/ among single malts from different casks is done mainly to ensure that the characteristics of the distillery's Single Malt Scotch will remain consistent across bottlings and through time.

Double Cask Single Malt Scotch

This is Single Malt Scotch that has been aged or matured in two different casks. For instance, a 12-year Double Cask Single Malt Scotch may have spent the first 10 years of its maturation phase aging in a Bourbon cask and the last 2 years in a Sherry cask.

Double casking is usually done to imbue a Single Malt Scotch with aromas, flavors, and other characteristics desired by the distillery's master blender.

Cask Strength Single Malt Scotch

This is Single Malt Scotch Whisky that has been bottled at cask-level alcoholic strength. In other words, the Single Malt Scotch was not diluted with water prior to bottling; thus, its bottling alcoholic strength is equivalent to its alcoholic strength in the cask.

Vintage Single Malt Scotch

Vintage Single Malt Scotch is a bottling of single malts with the same distillation year. It usually has a vintage year statement on the label—e.g., Distilled 1975. This vintage year statement must be in the same field of vision as the whisky's bottling year (if the whisky spent the years between the distillation year and the bottling year aging in the approved manner) or the whisky's age statement (e.g., aged 18 years).

Rare Single Malt Scotch

The term "Rare Single Malt Scotch Whisky" can refer to a limited-edition bottling or to a very old Single Malt Scotch, say 20 to 60 years old (distilleries normally bottle Single Malt Scotch at 10 to 12 years). Rare single malts are typically available at very limited quantities. Since they are rather exclusive and hard to find, they are usually very expensive.

Coastal Single Malt Scotch

This is Single Malt Scotch Whisky that has been aged in an excise warehouse near the sea. This description is typically used to refer to single malts from coastal distilleries.

Coastal single malts are often described as having sea flavors (e.g., seaweed) or as being salty on the palate. This is deemed to be the influence of the nearby seawater. The air from the sea penetrates the oak casks where the whisky is maturing, and this supposedly imbues the Scotch with unique flavors.

Chill-Filtered Single Malt Scotch

This is Single Malt Scotch Whisky that has undergone chill filtration. Prior to bottling and generally after water dilution, the Single Malt Scotch Whisky is chilled (usually to plus or minus 0 °C) then passed through filtering sheets. The chilling stage ensures that the fatty and oily compounds that are clouding up the whisky will clump up, making them easier to remove during the actual filtration stage.

Non-chill-filtered Single Malt Scotch

This is Single Malt Scotch Whisky that has NOT undergone chill filtration. This is not as clear or bright as chill-filtered single malts, but they generally have richer and more intense flavors and aromas.

Double Distilled Single Malt Scotch

This is Single Malt Scotch Whisky that has undergone double distillation. The first distillation occurs in the wash still; at this point, the wash is converted into low wines. The second distillation takes place in a spirit still; at this stage, the low wines are converted into new make or raw whisky, which is then casked or barreled for aging.

Triple Distilled Single Malt Scotch

This is Single Malt Scotch that has undergone triple distillation instead of the double distillation that is the standard among Single Malt Scotch Whisky distilleries. Triple-distilled Single Malt Scotch Whiskies are often lighter and cleaner than the typical, double-distilled Single Malt Scotch. They also often have higher ABV. Auchentoshan is an example of a triple-distilled Single Malt Scotch; Auchentoshan single malts go through an intermediate still after wash still distillation and before spirit still distillation.

Endnotes

1   Wishart, David. (2002). *Whisky Classified: Choosing Single Malts by Flavour*. London: Pavillion Books.

2   LaPointe, François-Joseph and Legendre, Pierre. (1994). A Classification of Pure Malt Scotch Whiskies. Applied Statistics, 43(1), 237-257. Date accessed: July 30, 2011 (http://adn.biol.umontreal.ca/~numericalecology/Reprints/Appl%20Stat%2043,%201994.pdf).

3   The Single Malt Whisky Flavour Map shown in this chapter has been prepared with and endorsed by the independent whisky expert David Broom, together with Diageo Scotland Ltd. The map features many brands of malt whisky, some of which are owned by and are

registered trade marks of Diageo Scotland Ltd, and some of which are owned by (and may be registered trade marks of) other companies. In addition to the names of individual distilleries listed on the Flavour Map, the Flavour Map device and associated logos are trade marks. Diageo © 2009

4   The Scotch Whisky Regulations 2009, S.I.2009/2890, Regulation 10(7). Date accessed: July 30, 2011 (http://www.legislation.gov.uk/uksi/2009/2890/regulation/10/made).

5   Scotch Whisky Association. (n.d.). *Highland Malt.* Date accessed: July 30, 2011 (http://www.scotch-whisky.org.uk/swa/241.html). Note that this list does not include Abhainn Dearg, although this distillery is an active distillery located on the Isle of Lewis, which is officially part of the Highland Region.

6   Scotch Whisky Association. (n.d.). *Lowland Malt.* Date accessed: July 31, 2011 (http://www.scotch-whisky.org.uk/swa/243.html).

7   The Scotch Whisky Regulations 2009, S.I.2009/2890, Regulation 10(6). Date accessed: July 31, 2011 (http://www.legislation.gov.uk/uksi/2009/2890/regulation/10/made).

8   Scotch Whisky Association. (n.d.). *Speyside Malt.* Date accessed: July 31, 2011 (http://www.scotch-whisky.org.uk/swa/244.html).

9   Scotch Whisky Association. (n.d.). *Islay Malt.* Date accessed: July 31, 2011 (http://www.scotch-whisky.org.uk/swa/242.html).

10 Scotch Whisky Association. (n.d.). *Campbeltown.* Date accessed: July 31, 2011 (http://www.scotch-whisky.org.uk/swa/523.html).

•Chapter VI•

Mixology and Single Malt Scotch Whisky

In the previous chapter, we discussed the propriety of drinking Single Malt Scotch "long"—that is, drinking Single Malt Scotch mixed with other beverages like soft drinks. In this chapter, we are featuring Single Malt Scotch Cocktails.

Whatever your stand may be on using Single Malt Scotch as a mixer, I'm sure you will love the recipes featured in this chapter. I'm also certain your friends will appreciate being given a choice—do they prefer their Scotch neat or long—the next time you have them over for Cocktails or a party.

Before we proceed to the whisky recipes, let me first give you a very brief background on mixology.

MIXOLOGY

According to Merriam-Webster. com, mixology is *the art or skill of preparing mixed drinks.*[1] Conventional wisdom and mainstream practice dictate that mixology is all about alcoholic mixed drinks—i.e., Cocktails. However, the very definition of the term "mixology" tells us that this discipline can actually encompass non-alcoholic mixed drinks.

Be that as it may, let it be clear that we are mainly concerned with the alcoholic variety in this chapter.

The History of Mixology

Mixed drinks B.C.

Mixed drinks seem to have ancient roots. In a tomb in Gordion, Turkey, archaeologists discovered drinking vessels that contained traces of what appeared to be a mixture of grape wine, honey wine (a.k.a. mead), and barley beer.[2]

This Gordion tomb was originally thought to be the final resting place of King Midas. Refinements in radiocarbon dating technology/techniques, however, have pushed back the approximate date of the tomb to 740 B.C.[3] This dates back to a time before King Midas's rule. Thus, the tomb is now ascribed to a different monarch, probably King Midas's father or grandfather.

Whatever the case, it is not important for our purposes

whose remains lie in the tomb in Gordion; what is important is that this Gordion tomb proves that mixed alcoholic drinks existed in ancient times.

Punch–before there were cocktails

The popularity of distilled spirits supposedly influenced the rise in popularity of mixed drinks.[4] Apparently, the harshness of distilled spirits meant people found it preferable (perhaps even necessary) to mix distilled spirits with other drinks and ingredients to blunt their sharpness and make them more, let's just say "manageable."

In the realm of mixed drinks made with distilled spirits, Punch used to reign supreme. Punch is an alcoholic drink that was traditionally prepared in bowls and made using five main ingredients.* The traditional Punch had the following ingredients (Wondrich, 2005, pp. 17-18):[5]

- Water
- Citrus fruits (e.g., lemon, lime, or citrons)

---

* Traditional Punch has five ingredients; some people made and drank Punch with fewer than five ingredients. Punch may have derived its name from the Hindi word for five, panch, but the number of ingredients does not appear to be the essence of Punch. For instance, if spices were unavailable, people would still be able to enjoy an unspiced Punch.

- Cane sugar
- Arrack, which is a type of spirit distilled from rice, palm sap, or sugar cane[**]
- Spice (e.g., tea, nutmeg, ambergris[***])

Wilson (2010), in his article "Spirits: Restoring dignity to Punch," gave an apt description of Punch (or conventional Punch) when he said that it is a combination of "strong (liquor), weak (water), sweet (sugar), sour (citrus), and spice."[6]

Punch is not originally an English drink. The fact that the alcoholic base of the traditional Punch is a distilled spirit not commonly found in England supports this.

The term "Punch" is assumed to have originated from "Panch," which is Hindi for "five" and is a reference to the number of ingredients that go into a bowl.[7-8] According to John Fryer (1698, p. 157), the naming tradition that gave Punch its name is akin to physicians naming their composition *Diapente* if such a composition has five ingredients (this is implied, not explicitly mentioned by Fryer) or *Diatesseron* if such a composition has four ingredients (this is explicitly mentioned).[9]

Today, Punch is no longer the Grand Dame of mixed drinks company—the Cocktail now has that honor—but it is still the first-ever mixed drink with a distilled spirit base.[****] In fact, Punch may have even paved the way for Cocktails; perhaps it was Punch that made people more accepting of the combination of flavors found in Cocktails.

Jeremiah P. Thomas (more popularly known as Jerry Thomas), the father of American mixology, must have felt the same way. In his pioneering book on American Cocktails, *How to Mix Drinks*,

---

[**] In England, some people replaced arrack—by need or by preference—with rum and brandy. Some used a combination of wines and spirit (wine and brandy, for instance). Punch made of arrack therefore became known as arrack or 'rack Punch.

[***]Ambergris is clotted whale cholesterol.

[****] It must be noted, though, that Punch evolved through time to incorporate other types of alcoholic ingredients. Traditional Punch had an arrack base, but Punch with a rum or brandy base was also common (as well as less expensive). Later on, Punch recipes with a base of whisky/whiskey, wine or wine-spirit combos also appeared.

or the Bon-Vivant's Companion, Thomas devoted an entire section to Punch. This section contained 75 different Punch recipes, including two variants of Brandy Punch, two variants of English Milk Punch, three variants of Gin Punch, and two variants of Regent's Punch. He also wrote the following tip on preparing Punch:

"To make punch of any sort in perfection, the ambrosial essence of the lemon must be extracted by rubbing lumps of sugar on the rind, which breaks the delicate little vessels that contain the essence, and at the same time absorbs it. This, and making the mixture sweet and strong, using tea instead of water, and thoroughly amalgamating all the compounds, so that the taste of neither the bitter, the sweet, the spirit, nor the element, shall be perceptible one over the other, is the grand secret, only to be acquired by practice.

In making hot toddy or hot punch, you must put in the spirits before the water: in cold punch, grog, & c., the other way.

The precise portions of spirit and water, or even of the acidity and sweetness, can have no general rule, as scarcely two persons make punch alike."[10]

The dawn of the cocktail

The Cocktail is the alcoholic mixed drink of choice today. It is a distinctly American invention and is the undeniable focus of modern mixology.

It is not clear how it got its name. Various "why it is named Cocktail" stories exist. In one story, the word Cocktail is derived from the name of a Mexican princess, Coctel.[11] In another, the word Cocktail is a mispronunciation of "coquetier," the French word for egg cup; apparently, Antoine Peychaud (of the Peychaud bitters fame) used egg cups to serve his Sazeracs (a classic Cocktail).[12]

Whatever the true origin of the word Cocktail, the earliest reference to it in print was made in the New Hampshire newspaper, *Farmer's Cabinet*. In this newspaper's April 28, 1803 issue, a spoof appeared, implying that a Cocktail is a good hangover cure.[13]

The earliest known definition of Cocktail, on the other hand, appeared in the newspaper, *The Balance and Columbian Repository* in 1806. Apparently, there was an election in the town of Claverack in New York, and, in the newspaper's May 6, 1806 issue, there was a humorous piece showing a losing candidate's Loss-and-Gain statement. It depicted how the candidate had gained nothing but had instead suffered numerous losses; aside from the election (the obvious loss), his losses included specific quantities of alcoholic beverages (e.g., rum-grogs, brandy-grogs, gin-slings, bitters) including 25 glasses of cock-tail.[14]

Following the May 6th issue, a reader responded with a letter asking for a clarification on what constitutes a Cock-tail. The reader's letter was posted in the newspaper's May 13, 1806 issue, and underneath was posted the editor's satirical yet informative response.

A Cock-tail, according to *The Balance and Columbian Repository* editor, is:

"a stimulating liquor, composed of spirits of any kind, sugar, water and bitters it is vulgarly called a bittered sling, and is supposed to be an excellent electioneering potion inasmuch as it renders the heart stout and bold, at the same time that it fuddles the head. It is said also, to be of great use to a democratic candidate: because, a person having swallowed a glass of it, is ready to swallow any thing else."[15]

Aside from being an obvious dig (and a very entertaining one at that) at politicians in general and the Democrats in particular, this definition is wonderful in its precision and exactness. It clearly states a Cocktail's essential components, and it is for this reason that today—more than two centuries after its conception—this 19th century definition of Cocktail remains relevant.

Cocktails got cold

In the early 19th century, when ice became readily available even in the summer months, bartenders started experimenting with iced Cocktail recipes. The Cocktail consumers loved them and cold mixed drinks soon became standard in Cocktail bars.

Cocktail fancy pants

Around this time (early 19th century), bartenders started innovating the standard preparation of drinks by experimenting on various Cocktail formulations, developing their own ingredients, and cultivating their showmanship skills to impress their customers and guests.

One of the most lasting developments during this time is the made-to-order Cocktail—where the customer placed an order for a specific Cocktail and the bartender whipped it up in front of the customer, all the while making small talk to ensure that his customer is kept entertained.

Cocktails, in turn, became fancier and more glamorous (with equally fancy and glamorous names). Cordials—sweet liqueurs—replaced sugar. Cocktails got garnishes. Cocktail glasses got chilled, rimmed with sugar or salt, and/or decorated with fruit wedges. Gone were the days when a bartender could simply add ice to a drink and the Cocktail would be "ready to drink." Instead, Cocktails might have to be strained, shaken (not stirred)—perhaps even juggled and twirled—to satisfy the fancy Cocktail customer.

Of course, fancy Cocktail bars also proliferated as a result, so did "performing bartenders" (i.e., bartenders who used various means—fancy tools, exaggerated and quick movements as well as other techniques—to entertain their guests). This new breed of bartenders turned mixing drinks into a performance worthy of high praise and generous salaries as well as tips.

The father of mixology

Jerry Thomas is considered to be the father of American mixology, acknowledged for his great contribution to the art and study of mixing drinks. Professor Jerry, as he was fondly called, operated his own bars. He also traveled around the U.S. (and even went to Europe), tending bars at hotels and saloons and—in the process—inadvertently promoted the Cocktail and fueled its rise in popularity.

A major part of his success can be attributed to his unique showmanship. He excelled in entertaining his guests—he put drinks on fire (e.g., his signature Cocktail, the *Blue Blazer*), he juggled, and he carried with him and used fancy bar tools. You can say he was one of the pioneers in flair bartending.

Jerry Thomas's biggest contribution to the field of mixology, however, is his book, *How to Mix Drinks or The Bon Vivant's Companion*, which was published in 1862. At that time, this was the most comprehensive and authoritative guide to mixed drinks. Not only did it include classic Cocktail recipes, it also included recipes of mixed drinks that Jerry Thomas himself developed. More importantly, it laid out the principles of mixing drinks.

All in all, this book probably contributed to the Cocktail's meteoric rise to fame. It is reasonable to suppose that as more and more people learned how to mix drinks, more and more people got to know Cocktails and acquired a taste for them.

Smooth vermouth and smoother operators

Around the 1870s, vermouth became a popular Cocktail ingredient or mixer.[16] Vermouth is fortified wine flavored with herbs (one of the most popular of which was wormwood). It gave bartenders a great way to reduce the harshness of Cocktail drinks. Vermouth's great flavor led to the development of lighter, smoother concoctions, such as the Martini and the Manhattan.

Around the same time, the standard method for preparing and mixing drinks changed nature once more. Exaggerated drink-pouring and juggling were gradually superseded by more elegant, professional movements. Bartenders still "performed" in a way—customers, after all, still watched as bartenders made drinks; however, they did so now with more refinement, elegance, and subtlety.

During and after prohibition

As the popularity of Cocktails rose, the opposition to alcohol consumption grew as well, culminating in the ratification of the *Eighteenth Amendment to the United States Constitution* on January 16, 1919. This amendment (effective January 17, 1920) made it illegal to make, sell, and transport alcoholic drinks within the U.S. as well as to import into and export from the U.S. such alcoholic beverages.

Prohibition simply drove alcohol consumption underground. Speakeasies, illegal watering holes where patrons had to "speak easy" to avoid drawing the attention of the authorities, flourished. Cocktails remained popular and, as a result of Prohibition, drinking them probably became even more fun. Organized crime rings profited from illegally distributing and importing alcohol. Americans who had money traveled abroad where they could freely indulge in alcoholic mixed drinks.

Soon, it became obvious that the national prohibition on alcohol consumption only succeeded in lining the pockets of crooks and not much else. In the end, the national prohibition on alcohol was lifted through the ratification on December 5, 1933 of the Twenty-first Amendment to the United States Constitution. Aside from repealing the Eighteenth Amendment, the Twenty-first Amendment essentially gave the individual states control over prohibiting or allowing alcohol manufacture, sales, transportation, importation, and export in their territories.

After Prohibition, Cocktail bars resumed legal operations. Bartending schools also flourished. However, the quality of instruction to be had from these post-Prohibition schools was less than ideal; so was the quality of the ingredients.[17] World War II did not help improve matters. Consequently, Cocktails became less refined and less special; the Cocktail started falling from its pedestal and preparing mixed drinks became less of an art and more of a task.

The mixed drinks renaissance and today's mixologists

Fortunately for the field of mixology, some chefs in the late 20th century started a new trend: that of using local, fresh ingredients and traditional methods in preparing food. This movement in the culinary world sparked a similar trend in the field of mixology, which led to the revival of good, solid principles of mixed-drink preparation and the renaissance of the art of preparing Cocktails.

Today, the art of mixing drinks continues to flourish and grow. Today's mixologists are the equivalent of pre-Prohibition mixed-drink artists in the amount of care they give to choosing and preparing their ingredients. They have successfully brought back the classic methods of mixed-drink preparation, even as they continue innovating new Cocktail recipes and experimenting on improving old techniques.

One of the most noteworthy among modern-day mixologists is Tony Abou-Ganim (The Modern Mixologist), without whom mixology would not be what it is today. World-class master mixologists like Francesco Lafranconi, Bridget Albert, Dale DeGroff, Simon Ford, Bobby "G" Gleason, Sasha Petraske, and Charlotte Voisey also deserve our thanks for leading the way to mixology's revival.

For today's mixologists, there can be no shortcuts, no subpar ingredients—and because of this, the art of mixing drinks has been fully revived and mixology is once again an art and a discipline to which one can be proud of belonging.

Mixologists and Bartenders – What Is the Difference?

Is mixology the same as bartending or, more to the point, are mixologists the same as bartenders? The answer varies, depending on whom you ask.

There are those who say bartending and mixology are just two faces of the same coin; they are simply two different names for the same craft, and one just happens to be fancier than the other. Likewise, there are those who say mixology and bartending are similar but not identical; both have to do with mixed alcoholic drinks, but mixology requires greater skills and a solid, knowledge base while bartending involves making and serving Cocktails.

So which version is true? Generally, bartending refers to the act of mixing drinks or Cocktails, while mixology is the study and creation of these Cocktails.

Mixologists have a deep knowledge of alcoholic beverages. They know their wines, tequila, gin, brandy, bourbon, Scotch; they know their bitters, ginger ale, and other liquors. More important, they know how these spirits and liquors react when combined at specific proportions in a Cocktail. They also know exactly which ingredients and mixing methods to use to attain specific flavor profiles. It is for this reason that mixologists are able to create their own Cocktails and innovate existing Cocktail recipes. Sometimes, mixologists even create their own ingredients.

Bartenders, on the other hand, mainly make Cocktail drinks. Typically, they follow the recipes that mixologists have invented or innovated.

This differentiation between bartenders and mixologists is likely to draw a lot of criticism. After all, there are those who call themselves bartenders— and have called themselves that all their lives—but serve Cocktails they themselves invented and created. Some of these veteran bartenders also probably know more about Cocktails than younger mixologists.

There's actually an easy way of getting over this impasse. Whatever one is called if he/she is passionate about mixed drinks, has made an extensive study of the art and science of mixing drinks and mixed drinks' ingredients, and creates Cocktail recipes based on this knowledge and experience, then that person is—in truth—a mixologist.

LAFRANCONI SCOTCH COCKTAILS

Master Mixologist Francesco Lafranconi was kind enough to share his very own Scotch whisky recipes. Here they are—enjoy!

Speyside Dram

What you need

1.5 oz. (4.5 cl) *Glenrothes Single Malt Scotch*

0.75 oz. (2.2 cl) Drambuie Honey Liqueur

0.5 oz. (1.5 cl) Fresh Squeezed Lemon Juice

5 Mint leaves

What to do

Shake all ingredients with ice and strain into a chilled cocktail glass.

Garnish: Lemon twist

Blood & Sand (classic)

What you need

1 oz. (3 cl) *Chivas Regal 12 yrs.*
0.75 oz. (2.2 cl) Cinzano Sweet Vermouth
0.75 oz. (2.2 cl) Luxardo Cherry Brandy
0.75 oz. (2.2 cl) Orange Juice

What to do

Shake all ingredients with ice and strain into a chilled cocktail glass.

Garnish: Orange twist

Horse's Neck (classic)

What you need

1.5 oz. (4.5 cl) Glenmorangie
2 dashes Angostura bitters
Fill up with ginger ale

What to do

Pour Scotch over ice in a highball glass. Fill to top with ginger ale with 2 dashes Angostura bitters. Stir and serve.

Garnish: Lemon peel and sprig of mint.

Tip: Use a peeler to cut the peel from a lemon lengthwise.

Perfect Rob Roy (classic)

What you need

2 oz. (6 cl) *Johnnie Walker Black Scotch Blended Whisky*
0.25 oz. (0.7 cl) Cinzano Sweet Vermouth
0.25 oz. (0.7 cl) Cinzano Dry Vermouth
1-2 Dashes Angostura Bitters

What to do

Stir all ingredients over ice in a mixing glass. Strain over ice into a chilled cocktail glass.

Garnish: Cocktail cherry

Bowmore Me Crazy

What you need

1.5 oz. (4.5cl) Bowmore 12 yr. Single Malt Scotch
0.5 oz. (1.5 cl) Kahlua Coffee Liqueur
0.5 oz. (1.5 cl) Mathilde Raspberry Liqueur

What to do

Stir all ingredients over ice in a mixing glass. Strain over ice into a rocks glass. Top with a layer of fresh cream.

Garnish: Cinnamon sugar rim

Jiggered Grouse

What you need

1.5 oz. (4.5 cl) *The Famous Grouse Blended Scotch*

0.5 oz. (1.5 cl) Harvey Bristol Cream Sherry

0.5 oz. (1.5 cl) King's Ginger Liqueur

0.5 oz. (1.5 cl) Apple Juice

0.5 oz. (1.5 cl) Fresh Lemon Juice

2 Dashes of Angostura Bitters

What to do

Shake first 5 ingredients with ice. Strain over ice into a highball glass. Top with bitters.

Garnish: Lemon peel and candied ginger

Cashmere Coffee

What you need

0.75 oz. (2.2 cl) *Cragganmore 12 yr. Single Malt Scotch*

0.75 oz. (2.2 cl) Grand Marnier

0.75 oz. (2.2 cl) Baileys Original Irish Cream Caramel-flavored

4 oz. (12 cl) Hot brewed Coffee

Float of lightly whipped cream

What to do

Rinse a tempered glass with hot water and pour the liquors and the coffee. Stir and layer the cream atop.

Garnish: An orange zest and sprinkle of ground cardamom

Endnotes

1   Mixology. (n.d.). In *Merriam-Webster.com*. Merriam-Webster, Incorporated. Date accessed: October 15, 2012 (http://www.merriam-webster.com/dictionary/mixology).

2   MSNBC.com. (December 17, 2009). Cheers! Eight ancient drinks uncorked by science. Date accessed: June 18, 2012 (http://technology-science.newsvine.com/_news/2009/12/17/-3645791-cheers-eight-ancient-drinks-uncorked-by-science).

3   Wilford, John Noble. (December 25, 2001). So Who Is Buried in Midas' Tomb? Date accessed: June 18, 2012 (http://www.nytimes.com/2001/12/25/health/so-who-is-buried-in-midas-tomb.html).

4   BarSmartsTV. (May 6, 2011). History of Mixology. Date accessed: June 18, 2012 (http://www.youtube.com/watch?v=7JDdQqTUl2c).

5   Wondrich, David. (2005). "A Brief History of Punch." In Anistatia Miller (Ed.), *Mixologist: The Journal of the American Cocktail* (pp. 15-34). New York, NY: Jared Brown.

6   Wilson, Jason. (November 9, 2010). Spirits: Restoring dignity to punch. Date accessed: June 18, 2012 (http://www.washingtonpost.com/wp-dyn/content/article/2010/11/09/AR201011-0904671.html).

7   Wilson, Jason. (November 9, 2010). Spirits: Restoring dignity to punch. Date accessed: June 18, 2012 (http://www.washingtonpost.com/wp-dyn/content/article/2010/11/09/AR201011-0904671.html).

8   Fryer, John. (1698). *A New Account of India and Persia in Eight Letters Being Nine Years Travels, Begun 1672 and Finished 1681.* Date accessed: September 27, 2012 (http://archive.org/stream/.)

9   Fryer, John. (1698). A New Account of India and Persia in Eight Letters Being Nine Years Travels, Begun 1672 and Finished 1681. Date accessed: September 27, 2012 (http://archive.org/stream/anewaccounteast-00whit-goog#page/n193/mode/2up).

10   Thomas, Jerry. (1862). How to Mix Drinks, or the Bon-Vivant's Companion. Date accessed: October 14, 2012 (http://archive.org/stream/howtomixdrink-so00schugoog#page/n15/mode/2up).

11   Bar Solution. (n.d.). Mixology: Introduction to Mixology and Its History. Date accessed: June 18, 2012 (http://www.bar-solution.com/BarManual_Sample.pdf).

12   Bar Solution. (n.d.). Mixology: Introduction to Mixology and Its History. Date accessed: June 18, 2012 (http://www.bar-solution.com/BarManual_Sample.pdf).

13   Graham, Colleen. (n.d.). What is a Cocktail? What is the History of the Cocktail? Date accessed: June 18, 2012 (http://cocktails.about.com/od/history/a/cocktail_dfntn.htm).

14   The Museum of the American Cocktail. (n.d.). The Origin of the Cocktail. Date accessed: June 18, 2012 (http://www.museumoftheamericancocktail.org/museum/thebalance.html).

15   The Museum of the American Cocktail. (n.d.). The Origin of the Cocktail. Date accessed: June 18, 2012 (http://www.museumoftheamericancocktail.org/museum/thebalance.html).

16   BarSmartsTV. (May 6, 2011). History of Mixology. Date accessed: June 18, 2012 (http://www.youtube.com/watch?v=7JDdQqTUI2c).

17   BarSmartsTV. (May 6, 2011). History of Mixology. Date accessed: June 18, 2012 (http://www.youtube.com/watch?v=7JDdQqTUI2c).

•Chapter VII•

Single Malt Scotch Whisky Distilleries

This chapter is simply an enumeration of all Single Malt Scotch distilleries, including those that are actively producing whisky, those that are permanently closed, and those that have been deactivated.

Note: Deactivated distilleries are temporarily closed distilleries. They are currently not operating; you could say that they are closed until further notice. Even though they are closed, however, their equipment and facilities remain and are kept in good, operating condition. Unlike permanently closed distilleries (the equipment and other facilities of which have most likely been sold or are not being maintained in good condition), deactivated distilleries can readily resume operations if needed or if management decides to do so. (Deactivated distilleries are usually referred to as mothballed distilleries.)

For the sake of simplicity, I will use "closed" distilleries to refer to both "permanently closed" distilleries and "deactivated distilleries" in this chapter.

Why read this chapter? It is to *Master Scotch,* so you can gain encyclopedic knowledge with which to impress fellow lovers of Single Malt Scotch, of course!

Seriously though, this chapter will help you gain a better understanding of your favorite spirit. The list of distilleries should give you an idea about how much variety there is in Single Malt Scotch Whisky. The regional classification of distilleries should give you a geographical point of reference and help you properly "place" the distilleries in your mental map of Scotland. The distilleries' production capacities should help you appreciate just how large a volume of whisky Scotland produces. The fact that water source information (when available) is included should also clue you in on how important water quality is to the production of whisky; in fact, the contamination of a distillery's water source could induce a distillery to stop operations.

This chapter will also give you an overview of Scotland's single malt whisky industry as a whole. By looking at the ownership information of distilleries, you will realize that more and more malt distilleries have become concentrated into the hands of conglomerates. This (and the considerable number of closed distilleries) should give you a new appreciation for those distilleries that remain independent today.

At the very least, this chapter will give you a handy list of Scotland's active and closed malt distilleries that you can refer to as needed. The list of closed distilleries is particularly important. There is the obvious historical value. Closed distilleries are a good subject for anyone who is keen on Single Malt Scotch, particularly those who love the history of this spirit. There is nostalgia involved, too. A whisky from a closed distillery could have been your first introduction to Single Malt Scotch. It could also have been your father's or your grandfather's favorite dram.

There are practical reasons, too. A connoisseur must know his single malts, even single malts from closed and deactivated distilleries. There is also the fact that knowing the names of closed distilleries will keep you on the lookout for old brands to add to your collection. Single malts from closed distilleries are true collectibles; since they are out of the general circulation, they are typically rare, expensive, and therefore precious.

SCOTCH WHISKY REGION

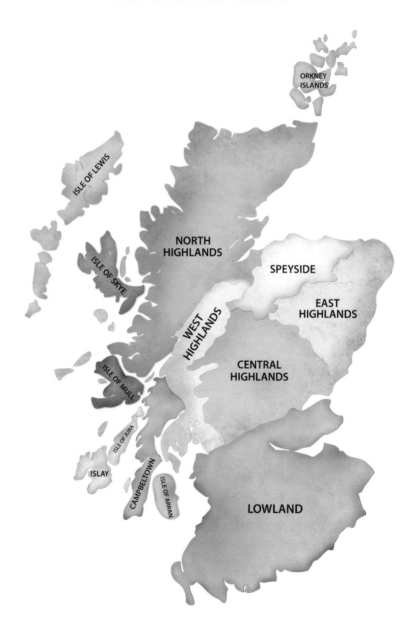

ORKNEY
ISLANDS

ISLE OF LEWIS

NORTH
HIGHLANDS

SPEYSIDE

ISLE OF SKYE

EAST
HIGHLANDS

WEST
HIGHLANDS

ISLE OF MULL

CENTRAL
HIGHLANDS

ISLE OF JURA

ISLAY

CAMPBELTOWN

ISLE OF ARRAN

LOWLAND

HIGHLAND (excluding Islands)

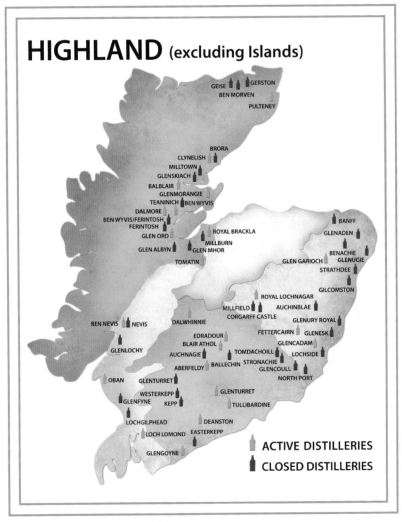

GEISE GERSTON
BEN MORVEN
PULTENEY

BRORA
CLYNELISH
MILLTOWN
GLENSKIACH
BALBLAIR
GLENMORANGIE
TEANINICH BEN WYVIS
DALMORE
BEN WYVIS/FERINTOSH
FERINTOSH
GLEN ORD
GLEN ALBYN
TOMATIN

BANFF
GLENADEN
ROYAL BRACKLA
MILLBURN
GLEN MHOR
BENACHIE
GLEN GARIOCH GLENUGIE
STRATHDEE

GILCOMSTON
ROYAL LOCHNAGAR
MILLFIELD AUCHINBLAE
CORGARFF CASTLE
GLENURY ROYAL
BEN NEVIS NEVIS DALWHINNIE
FETTERCAIRN GLENESK
EDRADOUR GLENCADAM
BLAIR ATHOL
GLENLOCHY
AUCHNAGIE TOMDACHOILL LOCHSIDE
ABERFELDY BALLECHIN STRONACHIE
GLENCOULL
OBAN GLENTURRET NORTH PORT
WESTERKEPP GLENTURRET
GLENFYNE KEPP
TULLIBARDINE
LOCHGILPHEAD DEANSTON
LOCH LOMOND EASTERKEPP
GLENGOYNE

▌ ACTIVE DISTILLERIES
🍶 CLOSED DISTILLERIES

LIST OF ACTIVE DISTILLERIES

Following is a list of the 100 actively operating (although not necessarily producing) Single Malt Scotch distilleries. The distilleries are classified according to region.

Important notes:

- See Chapter 5 for a comprehensive regional classification of Single Malt Scotch Whisky.
- In this chapter, the Islands are treated as a distinct whisky region, although it is officially part of the Highland Region.

HIGHLAND

There are 24 currently active distilleries in the Highland Region: 4 in the East, 9 in the North, 6 in the South, and 5 in the West. Overall, these 24 active Highland distilleries produce around 61,930,000 liters of Scotch whisky every year. Loch Lomond of the West Highlands contributes the largest portion (19% of the per-annum total) with its production capacity of 12,000,000 liters of alcohol per year.

Active EAST HIGHLANDS Distilleries

1. (Old) Fettercairn

Pronunciation: old FET-ter-kèrn
Founded: 1824
Ownership: (since 1973) Whyte & Mackay, a subsidiary of United Spirits Ltd.
Capacity: 1,600,000 liters of alcohol per year
Water Source: Grampian Mountain

The Fettercairn Distillery uses underground spring water sourced from the Grampian Mountains. This spring water is visibly free of suspended solids; in other words, the water looks clear when assessed with the naked eye. It has a metallic taste and an astringent mouthfeel, which is consistent with its high mineral content.

2. Glencadam

Pronunciation: glen CAdam
Founded: 1825
Ownership: (since 2003) Angus Dundee Distillers Plc
Capacity: 1,500,000 liters of alcohol per year
Water Source: The Moorans for distillation, Barry Burn for cooling

To distill its whisky, Glencadam pipes spring water from The Moorans, which is 8.7 miles away. Spring water from The Moorans is soft and pure—it has minimal salt and mineral content.

To cool alcoholic vapors so they will condense into liquid distillate, Glencadam draws water from the Barry Burn.

3. Glen Garioch

Pronunciation: glen GEEry
Founded: 1797
Ownership: (since 1970) Morrison Bowmore Distillers, a subsidiary of Suntory
Capacity: 1,000,000 liters of alcohol per year

Water Source: Spring water from Parcock Hills and Coutens Farm

Spring water from Parcock Hills is clear and of high quality, but its supply was not sufficient to meet the distillery's needs. For this reason, the distillery changed its main source of water to the spring in Coutens Farm—the Silent Spring of Coutens. The Coutens Farm spring enabled Glen Garioch to increase its production.

4. Lochnagar (Royal)

Pronunciation: lochnaGAR
Founded: 1845
Ownership: United Distillers and Vintners, a subsidiary of Diageo Plc
Capacity: 450,000 liters of alcohol per year
Water Source: Lochnagar Mountain

The Lochnagar Mountain is part of Scotland's Grampian Mountains. The springs found at the foot of this mountain supply the Royal Lochnagar Distillery with fresh, crystalclear water for distillation.

Active NORTH HIGH-LANDS Distilleries

1. Balblair

Pronunciation: balBLAIR
Founded: 1790
Ownership: (since 1996) Inver House Distillers, a subsidiary of Pacific Spirit (U.K.) Ltd., now part of International Beverage Holdings Limited (InterBev)
Capacity: 1,330,000 liters of alcohol per year
Water Source: Allt Dearg

Allt Dearg is Gaelic for "Red Burn." Edderton's Allt Dearg originates from the Struie Hills. The soft stream water then flows through an open peaty ditch to reach the Balblair Distillery, where it is used—untreated—in the whisky distillation process.

2. Clynelish

Pronunciation: KLEIN-lish or klein-LISH
Founded: 1819
Ownership: United Distillers and Vintners, a subsidiary of Diageo Plc
Capacity: 3,250,000 liters of alcohol per year

Water Source: Clynemilton Burn

Water from Clynemilton Burn, which is located over a mile north of the distillery, is transported to the Clynelish Distillery through a water pipeline. It is alleged that gold has been found at the head of this watercourse, and urban legend has it that there is actually still some gold to be "panned" in Clynemilton Burn.

3. Dalmore

Pronunciation: dalMORE
Founded: 1839
Ownership: Whyte & Mackay, a subsidiary of United Spirits Ltd.
Capacity: 4,200,000 liters of alcohol per year
Water Source: River Averon, also known as River Alness

The water of the River Alness comes from Loch Morie, a lake in Easter Ross, and flows into the sea loch of Cromarty Firth, on the northern shores of which lies the Dalmore Distillery. On its way from its source (the Loch Morie) to the Dalmore Distillery, the river passes through some peaty terrain—thus the brown color of the water used in Dalmore's distillation.

Dalmore draws water from the Alness River with the help of a weir (a small overflow dam set on the river to alter the flow of water) and a lade (a channel through which water flows from the river to the distillery). Water supply could be scarce when water levels fall (say, due to drought).

4. Glenmorangie

Pronunciation: glen-MO-ran-gie
Founded: 1843
Ownership: The Glenmorangie Company, a subsidiary of Moët Hennessy - Louis Vuitton
Capacity: 4,000,000 liters of alcohol per year
Water Source: Tarlogie Springs

Glenmorangie owns Tarlogie Springs as well as the land around it. Tarlogie spring water is very clear and hard. Its rich mineral content comes from the natural process it had to undergo before it could reach the surface. Apparently, Tarlogie spring water is century-old rainwater that has just spent the last 100 years being filtered through layers of limestone and sandstone before surfacing in the springs of Tarlogie.

5. Glen Ord (Singleton)

Pronunciation: glen ORD
Founded: 1838
Ownership: United Distillers and Vintners, a subsidiary of Diageo Plc
Capacity: 5,000,000 liters of alcohol per year
Water Source: Allt Fionnaidh and boreholes

The fresh water of the Allt Fionnaidh (White Burn in English) is a combination of waters from two lakes: Loch nan Eun (which gets its water from rain) and the Loch nam Bonnach (which gets its water from springs). Glen Ord also guarantees its supply of fresh water through boreholes that give direct access to an aquifer.

6. Pulteney

Pronunciation: Old PULT-nee
Founded: 1826
Ownership: (since 1995) Inver House Distillers, a subsidiary of Pacific Spirit (U.K) Ltd., now part of International Beverage Holdings Limited (InterBev)
Capacity: 1,000,000 liters of alcohol per year
Water Source: Loch Hempriggs

Old Pulteney gets process and cooling water directly from an open mill lade that channels water from the Loch Hempriggs to the distillery. Water from the Loch Hempriggs is naturally soft.

7. Royal Brackla

Pronunciation: BRACK-la
Founded: 1812
Ownership: (since 1998) John Dewar & Sons Ltd., a subsidiary of Bacardi Ltd.
Capacity: 2,500,000 liters of alcohol per year
Water Source: Cawdor Burn and springs on Cawdor Woods

Water in the Cawdor Burn is peat-brown in color.

8. Teaninich

Pronunciation: TEE-ah-nin-ik
Founded: 1817
Ownership: United Distillers and Vintners, a subsidiary of Diageo Plc
Capacity: 4,000,000 liters of alcohol per year
Water Source: Dairywell Spring

For its distillation and cooling purposes, Teaninich collects water from the nearby Dairywell Spring.

9. Tomatin

Pronunciation: TO-ma-tin or To-MA-tin
Founded: 1897
Ownership: The Tomatin Distillery Co. Ltd., a subsidiary of Takara Shuzo Co., Ltd.
Capacity: 5,000,000 liters of alcohol per year
Water Source: Alt-na-Frith

A tributary of the River Findhorn, passing through peat and heather and flowing over red granite, the Alt-na-Frith or Free Burn supplies the Tomatin Distillery with fresh mountain water from the Monadhliath (the Grey Mountains).

Active SOUTH HIGHLANDS Distilleries

1. Aberfeldy

Pronunciation: AberFELdy
Founded: 1896
Ownership: John Dewar & Sons Ltd., a subsidiary of Bacardi Ltd.
Capacity: 2,100,000 liters of alcohol per year
Water Source: Pitilie Burn

Aberfeldy uses hard water for distillation. This water (sourced from the Pitilie Burn) springs from hard, dark-colored rocks flecked with metals (specifically iron and gold) and passes over various types of vegetation.

2. Blair Athol

Pronunciation: blair ATHol
Founded: 1798
Ownership: United Distillers and Vintners, a subsidiary of Diageo Plc
Capacity: 2,000,000 liters of alcohol per year
Water Source: Allt Dour

The Allt Dour (Burn of the Otter) passes through the

grounds of the distillery. The crystal-clear water of this source originates from the slopes of the Ben Vrackie.

supplies soft water to the distillery that is on the spring water's path as it descends to the River Tummel.

3. Deanston

Pronunciation: DEENston
Founded: 1966
Ownership: (since 1990) Burn Stewart Distillers Ltd., now part of Distell
Capacity: 3,000,000 liters of alcohol per year
Water Source: River Teith

Streams located in the Trossachs feed the River Teith soft water that has been naturally filtered through granite and has flowed over peat deposits.

5. Glenturret

Pronunciation: glenTURret
Founded: 1959
Ownership: (since 1990) Highland Distillers, acquired by The Edrington Group
Capacity: 340,000 liters of alcohol per year
Water Source: Loch Turret and River Turret

For distillation, Glenturret pipes clean, clear, and soft water down from the Loch Turret on Ben Chonzie. For cooling, it uses water taken from the River Turret.

4. Edradour

Pronunciation: Ed-ra-dower
Founded: 1837
Ownership: (since 2002) Signatory Vintage
Capacity: 90,000 liters of alcohol per year
Water Source: Mhoulin Muir

A spring on Mhoulin Muir (which is on the Ben Vrackie)

6. Tullibardine

Pronunciation: Tully-bar-deen
Founded: 1949
Ownership: Tullibardine Distillery Ltd.
Water Source: 2,500,000 liters of alcohol per year
Water Source: Danny Burn

Tullibardine gets its supply of soft water from the Danny

Burn, which flows past the distillery and is fed by a spring on Ochil Hills. Ochil Hills is famous for its pure, crystal-clear spring water; it is actually a water source for a leading brand of bottled water, Highland Spring.

was built, and, along the way, it collected and diverted water from traditional water sources, including the Mill Burn. Consequently, the Ben Nevis Distillery now uses water from Loch Treig piped through the hydro-electric tunnel.

Active WEST HIGHLANDS Distilleries

1. Ben Nevis

Pronunciation: ben Nevis
Founded: 1825
Ownership: (since 1989) Ben Nevis Distillery Ltd., a subsidiary of Nikka Whisky, owned by the Asahi Group
Capacity: 2,000,000 liters of alcohol per year
Water Source: Loch Treig

Ben Nevis used to get its distillation water from Allt a' Mhuilinn (Mill Burn), which is fed by two small lakes: Coire Na Ciste and Coire Leis. Upon the implementation of the Lochaber Hydro-Electric Power Scheme, however, a tunnel carrying water from the Loch Treig (Loch of Death) down the Ben Nevis (the mountain)

2. Dalwhinnie

Pronunciation: dal-WHIN-ee
Founded: 1897
Ownership: United Distillers and Vintners, a subsidiary of Diageo Plc
Capacity: 1,300,000 liters of alcohol per year
Water Source: Allt an t-Sluic

Allt an t-Sluic is the Dalwhinnie distillery's own burn. Its water comes from the Lochan na Doire-uaine (the Lake of the Green Wood or Grove), which is on Drumochter Hills and to which no distillery other than Dalwhinnie has usage rights. On its way from Drumochter Hills to Allt an t-Sluic, water from the lake of Doire Uaine goes underground and runs over peat and heather moors.

3. Glengoyne

Pronunciation: glen GOIN
Founded: 1833
Ownership: (since 2003) Ian Macleod Distillers Ltd.
Capacity: 1,100,000 liters of alcohol per year
Water Source: Dumgoyne Hill

The distillery pipes water from Dumgoyne Hill, which is part of the range of hills known as Campsie Fells. Water from Dumgoyne Hill is clean, clear, and soft.

4. Loch Lomond

Pronunciation: Loch Lowmond
Founded: 1966
Ownership: Loch Lomond Distillery Company Ltd.
Capacity: 12,000,000 liters of alcohol per year
Water Source: Loch Lomond

Loch Lomond has the largest surface area and second largest water volume among all freshwater lakes in Scotland. It supplies the distillery with soft water.

5. Oban

Pronunciation: Ow-b'n
Founded: 1794
Ownership: United Distillers and Vintners, a subsidiary of Diageo Plc
Capacity: 670,000 liters of alcohol per year
Water Source: Loch Gleann and Loch Bhearraidh

On its way to the distillery from Ardconnel, where the two lakes are located, the water from the lakes Gleann and Bhearraidh flows over fairly peaty terrain.

ISLANDS (part of Highland)

ISLE OF LEWIS

ORKNEY ISLANDS

STORNOWAY

ABHAINN DEARG

HIGHLAND PARK

SCAPA

ISLE OF SKYE

ISLE OF ARRAN

ARRAN

TALISKER

CORRY

ISLE OF JURA

BARRA

TOBERMORY   ISLE OF MULL

ISLE OF
JURA

ACTIVE DISTILLERIES

CLOSED DISTILLERIES

ISLANDS

There are eight active distilleries in the Islands region: one in the Isle of Lewis, one in the Isle of Barra, one in the Isle of Arran, one in the Isle of Jura, one in the Isle of Mull, two in Orkney Islands, and one in the Isle of Skye.

Overall, the Islands region produces around 9,470,000 liters of alcohol every year (excluding Barra's target production volume), with Highland Park contributing around 26% of the region's total yearly production capacity.

1. Abhainn Dearg

Pronunciation: Ah-veen Gee-rag
Founded: 2008
Ownership: Mark Tayburn
Location: Lewis
Capacity: 20,000 liters of alcohol per year
Water Source: Abhainn Dearg

The distillery takes its name from the river from which it sources its water for distillation, the Abhainn Dearg or the Red River. The river water comes from the mountain streams of Uig Hills, and it is soft and clear with little to no peat. It's also very clean due to the lack of houses and industrial activities around the river banks.

2. Isle of Arran

Pronunciation: isle of ARran
Founded: 1993
Ownership: (since 1993) Isle of Arran Distillers
Location: Arran
Capacity: 750,000 liters of alcohol per year
Water Source: Loch na Davie

The distillery uses soft and fresh water that springs on the slopes of the Beinn Bhreac; water from this source flows through granite (which purifies it) and peat on its way to the distillery.

3. Isle of Barra

Pronunciation: isle of barra
Founded: 2008
Ownership: Uisge Beatha Nan Eilean Ltd.
Location: Barra
Capacity: 25,000 liters of alcohol per year[1]
Water Source: Loch Uisge

Loch Uisge (which translates to Lake of Water in English) is the highest lake in Barra. Uisge Beatha Nan Eilean Ltd., which owns the Isle of Barra distillery, acquired this reservoir on November 29, 2005.

Note: The Isle of Barra distillery is yet to fill its first cask of Single Malt Scotch Whisky, although casks from its first two years of distillation have already been reserved. It plans to commence production as soon as construction of the distillery is completed.

---

[1] This is according to Andrew Currie, co-founder of the Isle of Barra distillery, who was quoted in a Stornoway Gazette article published on February 11, 2005. This article was accessed on December 26, 2012, at http://www.stornowaygazette.co.uk/news/local-headlines/plans-still-on-track-for-barra-distillery-1-115885.

4. Highland Park

Pronunciation: HIGHland park
Founded: 1798
Ownership: Highland Distillers, acquired by The Edrington Group
Location: Orkney
Capacity: 2,500,000 liters of alcohol per year
Water Source: Cattie Maggie's Well and Crantit Spring

Cattie Maggie's Well, which lies to the east of the distillery, is the distillery's traditional water source; it was also the water source of choice of Mansie Euson—Orkney's famous smuggler, who supposedly did some illegal distilling at the site where Highland Park currently stands. This pool with its hard, mineral-rich water is fed by underground springs. Crantit Spring lies to the west of the distillery, and, along the way, it passes through some marshy terrain; it, too, supplies the distillery with high-quality, hard water for distillation.

5. Isle of Jura

Pronunciation: isle of JUU-rah
Founded: 1963
Ownership: Whyte & Mackay, a subsidiary of United Spirits Ltd.
Location: Jura
Capacity: 2,200,000 liters of alcohol per year
Water Source: Loch a Bhaile Mhargaidh

The water of the Loch a Bhaile Mhargaidh (Market Loch) flows over rock and peat; it is characteristically soft, peaty, and dark.

6. Scapa

Pronunciation: SKAA-pa
Founded: 1885
Ownership: Chivas Brothers, a subsidiary of Pernod Ricard
Location: Orkney
Capacity: 1,000,000 liters of alcohol per year
Water Source: Springs at Orquil Farm

Peaty water is piped to the distillery from the springs found at Orquil Farm. Before bubbling through and flowing over peat bogs, this spring water flowed over various types of vegetation and was filtered through sandstone. Lingro Burn, beside which the distillery is situated, does not supply the distillery with process water; what it does is provide the distillery with cooling water.

7. Talisker

Pronunciation: TA-lis-ker
Founded: 1831
Ownership: United Distillers and Vintners, a subsidiary of Diageo Plc
Location: Skye
Capacity: 2,000,000 liters of alcohol per year
Water Source: Cnoc nan Speireag Burn

This water source provides the Talisker distillery with reddish water for distillation. This water has high peat content, amplified even more as it passes through peaty terrain on its way down Cnoc nan Speireag to the distillery.

8. Tobermory (Ledaig)[2]

Pronunciation: TO-ber-MORE-ee
Founded: 1798

Ownership: (since 2002) Burn Stewart Distillers Ltd., now part of Distell
Location: Mull
Capacity: 1,000,000 liters of alcohol per year
Water Source: A lake near Mishnish Lochs

The term Mishnish Lochs refers to a group of lochs that have been purposely interconnected or interlinked to make a reservoir. Near the Mishnish Lochs is a private lake with significantly peaty water that Tobermory uses for distillation.

[2]The Tobermory distillery produces two brands of Single Malt Scotch Whisky: the Tobermory and the Ledaig. The former (with its two variants: the 10-year-old Tobermory and the 15-year-old Tobermory) is smooth and light, while the Ledaig (with its single variant: the 10-year-old Ledaig) is highly peated.

LOWLAND

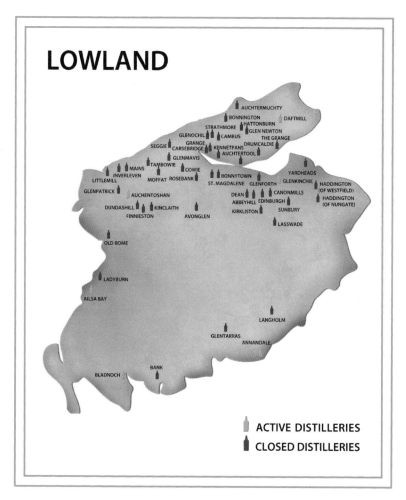

Map labels:

AUCHTERMUCHTY
BONNINGTON DAFTMILL
STRATHMORE HATTONBURN
GLENOCHIL GLEN NEWTON
CAMBUS THE GRANGE
SEGGIE GRANGE DRUMCALDIE
CARSEBRIDGE KENNETPANS
AUCHTERTOOL
GLENMAVIS
TAMBOWIE
MAINS COWIE YARDHEADS
INVERLEVEN BONNYTOWN GLENKINCHIE
LITTLEMILL MOFFAT ROSEBANK
ST. MAGDALENE GLENFORTH HADDINGTON (OF WESTFIELD)
GLENPATRICK DEAN CANONMILLS HADDINGTON (OF NUNGATE)
AUCHENTOSHAN ABBEYHILL EDINBURGH
DUNDASHILL KINCLAITH KIRKLISTON SUNBURY
FINNIESTON AVONGLEN LASSWADE
OLD ROME
LADYBURN
AILSA BAY
LANGHOLM
GLENTARRAS
ANNANDALE
BANK
BLADNOCH

ACTIVE DISTILLERIES
CLOSED DISTILLERIES

LOWLAND

There are six active distilleries in the Lowland Region (well, Annandale has reopened but has yet to fill its first cask). Active Lowlands distilleries (excluding Annandale) are capable of producing around 8,665,000 total liters of alcohol per year. That is less than the production capacity of the Highland distillery, Loch Lomond, or the Speyside distillery, Glenfiddich.

1. Ailsa Bay

Founded: 2007[i]
Ownership: William Grant & Sons Ltd.

Capacity: 5,000,000 liters of alcohol per year
Water Source: Penwhapple Reservoir

The Penwhapple Reservoir is one of the main sources of water for the locals and local industry.[ii]

2. Annandale

Founded: 1830[iii]
Ownership: Annandale Distillery Company[iv]
Capacity: Unknown
Water Source: Guillielands Burn[v] (or at least it was in the past)

Note: This distillery has just been acquired by the Annandale Distillery Company. According to the distillery's website, Annandale intends to produce significantly phenolic or smoky Single Malt Scotch Whisky, although they do plan to produce a non-phenolic malt whisky as well.

3. Auchentoshan

Pronunciation: OchunTOshun
Founded: 1825
Ownership: (since 1984) Morrison Bowmore Distillers, a subsidiary of Suntory
Capacity: 1,650,000 liters of alcohol per year
Water Source: Loch Katrine

Clear water for distillation is piped from Loch Katrine, a Highland lake (in the Trossachs, specifically) some 21 miles away from Auchentoshan.

4. Bladnoch

Pronunciation: BLADnoch
Founded: 1825
Ownership: (since 1994) Raymond Armstrong
Capacity: 250,000 liters of alcohol per year
Water Source: Loch Ma Berry

Although the Bladnoch distillery is situated on the bank of the River Bladnoch, it cannot get its water directly from its part of the river; the part of the river where the distillery is located is tidal. Instead, a watercourse directs water to the distillery from a weir on the River Bladnoch (this weir is a mile away from the distillery).

River Bladnoch's water comes from Loch Maberry, one of the lakes on the slopes of nearby Galloway Hills.

5. Daftmill

Founded: 2005 (granted license to distill)[vi]
Capacity: 65,000 litres[vii]
Ownership: Francis and Ian Cuthbert
Water Source: Artesian well on site

The distillery is sitting on a natural source of clean, clear process water; all it has to do is draw it up through layers of sand and gravel to the surface.

Note: This distillery distilled its first whisky on December 16, 2005. As of this writing, though, the distillery's website says its whisky is still maturing so it's not yet for sale.

Vintners, a subsidiary of Diageo Plc
Capacity: 1,700,000 liters of alcohol per year
Water Source: Spring water from Lammermuir Hills

The clear and hard water for distillation is sourced from a spring within the distillery premises. This spring, in turn, is fed by a reservoir in Lammermuir Hills.

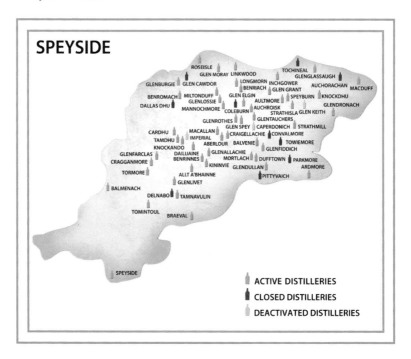

SPEYSIDE

ACTIVE DISTILLERIES
CLOSED DISTILLERIES
DEACTIVATED DISTILLERIES

6. Glenkinchie

Pronunciation: glen KIN-chee
Founded: 1837
Ownership: United Distillers and

SPEYSIDE

There are 51 active distilleries in the Speyside Region. Based on land area, Speyside is very small compared to the Highlands. Even so, it has twice as many active distilleries as the larger Highland Region. Its production capacity, which is approximately 168,590,000 liters per year, is also 172% larger than that of the Highlands. Speyside is, without any doubt, the most prolific whisky region in Scotland.

1. Aberlour

Pronunciation: ABER-louwer
Founded: 1826
Ownership: (since 2001) Chivas Brothers, a subsidiary of Pernod Ricard
Capacity: 3,500,000 liters of alcohol per year
Water Source: St. Drostan's Well

St. Drostan's Well, which is on the grounds of the distillery, supplies Aberlour distillery with soft spring water sourced from the Ben Rinnes Mountain.

2. Allt A'Bhainne

Pronunciation: olta-VAYne
Founded: 1975
Ownership: (since 1975) Chivas Brothers, a subsidiary of Pernod Ricard
Capacity: 4,000,000 liters of alcohol per year
Water Source: Scurran Burn & Rowantree Burn

Scurran and Rowantree Burns are fed by springs on the Ben Rinnes Mountain. The pure spring water passes through a natural filtration system on its way from the mountain to the burns. Natural filters include granite on the Ben Rinnes Mountain, and gravel on the bed of the burns themselves. Moreover, the vegetation and peat, over which the water flows on its way down the mountain, also imbue the water with distinct characteristics.

3. Ardmore

Pronunciation: ard-MORE
Founded: 1898
Ownership: Beam Global, owned by Fortune Brands
Capacity: 4,200,000 liters of alcohol per year
Water Source: Knockandy Hill Springs

The fresh, non-peaty water for distillation is piped into the distillery from several springs on Knockandy Hill.

4. Auchroisk (Singleton)

Pronunciation: othrUjsk
Founded: 1974
Ownership: United Distillers and Vintners, a subsidiary of Diageo Plc
Capacity: 3,100,000
Water Source: Dorie's Well & Mulben Burn

For distillation, the distillery uses the soft spring water from Dorie's Well, which can be found on site. Water from the nearby Mulben Burn is used only for cooling.

Note: In the past, this distillery bottled Single Malt Scotch Whisky under the brand "The Singleton" but the distillery now mainly produces Single Malt Scotch to be used for blends (specifically the J&B Blended Scotch Whisky). It has also moved away from "The Singleton" brand (or, to be more precise, "The Singleton of Auchroisk" brand) and is now using the distillery's name, Auchroisk, as its brand name.

5. Aultmore

Pronunciation: OLT-more
Founded: 1896

Ownership: John Dewar & Sons Ltd., a subsidiary of Bacardi Ltd.
Capacity: 2,900,000 liters of alcohol per year
Water Source: Auchinderran Burn

Auchinderran Burn is around a mile away from the distillery, and it is the "big burn" or "large river" to which the name of the distillery refers.

6. Balmenach

Pronunciation: balMEHnack
Founded: 1824
Ownership: (since 1997) Inver House Distillers, a subsidiary of Pacific Spirit (U.K.) Ltd., now part of International Beverage Holdings Limited (InterBev)
Capacity: 2,000,000 liters of alcohol per year
Water Source: Cromdale Hills

The clean spring water originates from the Cromdale Hills. It is then naturally filtered (through the surrounding landscape) on its way to the dams, from which the distillery takes its process water.

7. Balvenie

Pronunciation: balVEEnie
Founded: 1892
Ownership: (since 1892) William Grant & Sons Ltd.
Capacity: 5,600,000 liters of alcohol per year
Water Source: Robbie Dubh Burn (also known as Robbie Dhu Spring)

Robbie Dubh Burn, a tributary of the River Fiddich, provides the distillery with soft, peaty, granite-filtered spring water, which is delivered through pipes to ensure that it doesn't get contaminated on its way from the Conval Hills (where the burn is located) to the distillery. The distillery's owner (William Grant & Sons) actually owns the 1,200 acres of land around the Robbie Dubh; this is so access to the burn can be limited, further ensuring that the distillery's water source will remain pure.

8. BenRiach

Pronunciation: ben REE-ak
Founded: 1898
Ownership: BenRiach Distillery Company Ltd.
Capacity: 2,800,000 liters of alcohol per year
Water Source: Boreholes on site

BenRiach uses hard spring water drawn from deep underground through boreholes that have been drilled on site.

9. Benrinnes

Pronunciation: benRINnes
Founded: 1835
Ownership: United Distillers and Vintners, a subsidiary of Diageo Plc
Capacity: 2,600,000 liters of alcohol per year
Water Source: Scurran Burn & Rowantree Burn

Scurran and Rowantree Burns are fed by springs on the Ben Rinnes Mountain. The pure spring water passes through a natural filtration system on its way from the mountain to the burns. Natural filters include granite on the Ben Rinnes Mountain and gravel on the bed of the burns themselves. The vegetation and peat over which the water flows on its way down the mountain also imbue the water with distinct characteristics.

10. Benromach

Pronunciation: benROmach
Founded: 1898
Ownership: (since 1993) Gordon & MacPhail
Capacity: 500,000 liters of alcohol per year
Water Source: Chapelton Springs

A pipeline delivers spring water from the Romach Hills, specifically from the Chapelton Springs, down to the distillery.

11. Braeval

Pronunciation: BRAY-val
Founded: 1974
Ownership: Chivas Brothers, a subsidiary of Pernod Ricard
Capacity: 4,000,000 liters of alcohol per year
Water Source: Preenie & Kate's Wells, Pitilie Burn

Spring water sourced from the wells of Preenie and Kate serves as Braeval's process water, while hard water from the Pitilie Burn serves as the distillery's cooling water.

Note: Braeval doesn't sell Single Malt Scotch under its name, and most of its single malt whisky output goes into blends.

12. Cardhu

Pronunciation: car-DOO
Founded: 1824
Ownership: United Distillers and Vintners, a subsidiary of Diageo Plc
Capacity: 2,300,000 liters of alcohol per year
Water Source: Sources on Mannoch Hill

A pipeline approximately 2 miles long delivers soft spring water from the Mannoch Hill to the distillery.

13. Cragganmore

Pronunciation: CRAGganmore
Founded: 1870
Ownership: United Distillers and Vintners, a subsidiary of Diageo Plc
Capacity: 1,600,000
Water Source: Craggan Burn

The Craggan Burn, which originates from the Craggan More

Hill, provides the distillery with hard, mineral-rich spring water for distillation.

14. Craigellachie

Pronunciation: craiGELlachie
Founded: 1891
Ownership: (since 1998) John Dewar & Sons Ltd., a subsidiary of Bacardi Ltd.
Capacity: 2,700,000 liters of alcohol per year
Water Source: Blue Hill, River Fiddich

The distillery gets its process water from the Blue Hill dam, which, in turn, sources its water from a spring on Little Conval Hill. Water from the River Fiddich is used for cooling.

15. Dailuaine

Pronunciation: dale-YOU-an or dal-OO-ayn
Founded: 1852
Ownership: United Distillers and Vintners, a subsidiary of Diageo Plc
Capacity: 3,200,000 liters of alcohol per year
Water Source: Balliemullich Burn, Carron Burn

Clean water for distillation comes from the Balliemullich Burn, while water for cooling comes from the Carron Burn (which is right beside the distillery, although the distillery does get its cooling water from a dam on the burn a little bit upstream). Both burns are fed by water sources on the Ben Rinnes Mountain.

16. Dufftown (Singleton)

Pronunciation: DUFFtown
Founded: 1896
Ownership: United Distillers and Vintners, a subsidiary of Diageo Plc
Capacity: 4,000,000 liters of alcohol per year
Water Source: Jock's Well

Jock's Well supplies the distillery with exceptional spring water from the Conval Hills.

Note: The Single Malt Scotch Whisky of the Dufftown distillery is Diageo's "The Singleton" distributed in Europe (to be precise, it's "The Singleton of Dufftown"). It used to be that "The Singleton" referred to Single Malt Scotch from Diageo's Auchroisk distillery.

17. Glen Elgin

Pronunciation: glen ELgin
Founded: 1900
Ownership: United Distillers and Vintners, a subsidiary of Diageo Plc
Capacity: 1,800,000 liters of alcohol per year
Water Source: Local springs, Glen Burn

The soft water that Glen Elgin uses for distillation is sourced from springs in the loch of Millbuies area. Glen Burn feeds a reservoir that supplies the distillery with cooling water.

18. Glen Grant

Pronunciation: Glen Grant
Founded: 1840
Ownership: (since 2005) Campari
Capacity: 5,900,000 liters of alcohol per year
Water Source: Caperdonich Well

The clean spring water from the Caperdonich Well is piped to the Glen Grant distillery for process use.

19. Glen Moray

Pronunciation: glen murRAY
Founded: 1897
Ownership: (since 2008) La Martiniquaise
Capacity: 2,000,000 liters of alcohol per year
Water Source: Lossie River

The Lossie River is fed by the Loch Trevie. Glen Moray uses its water, which has a peat-brown tinge, for production.

20. Glen Spey

Pronunciation: glen SPEY
Founded: 1878
Ownership: United Distillers and Vintners, a subsidiary of Diageo Plc
Capacity: 1,400,000 liters of alcohol per year
Water Source: Doonie Burn, Rothes Burn

Clean water for distillation comes from the Doonie Burn, while water for cooling comes from the peaty-brown Rothes Burn.

21. Glenallachie

Pronunciation: glenALlakkee
Founded: 1967
Ownership: Chivas Brothers, a subsidiary of Pernod Ricard

Capacity: 2,800,000 liters of alcohol per year
Water Source: Sources on the Ben Rinnes mountain

Glenallachie uses spring water from the Ben Rinnes mountain.

22. Glenburgie

Pronunciation: glenBURgee
Founded: 1829
Ownership: (since 2005) Chivas Brothers, a subsidiary of Pernod Ricard
Capacity: 2,800,000
Water Source: Wells on site, Burgie Burn

Several wells on the distillery grounds guarantee Glenburgie a steady source of clean spring water for distillation, while a dam on the nearby Burgie Burn provides the distillery with cooling water.

Note: Glenburgie operated 2 Lomond stills from 1956 to 1981, and the malt whisky produced by these stills was bottled under the Glencraig brand.

23. GlenDronach

Pronunciation: glenDRONak
Founded: 1826
Ownership: (since 2008) Benriach Distillery Company Ltd.
Capacity: 1,300,000 liters of alcohol per year
Water Source: Local spring, Dronach Burn

Approximately four miles from the distillery lies the spring that supplies the distillery with process water. Right beside the distillery is the Dronach Burn, which supplies GlenDronach with cooling water.

24. Glendullan (Singleton)

Pronunciation: glenDULlan
Founded: 1898
Ownership: United Distillers and Vintners, a subsidiary of Diageo Plc
Capacity: 3,700,000 liters of alcohol per year
Water Source: Conval Hills

Spring water used for distillation comes from the Conval Hills.

Note: This is "The Singleton," or to be more precise "The Singleton of Glendullan," produced by Diageo for the U.S. market. It used to be that the brand name "The Singleton" referred to Auchroisk Single Malt Scotch Whisky.

25. Glenfarclas

Pronunciation: glenFARclas
Founded: 1836
Ownership: (since 1865) J. & G. Grant
Capacity: 3,000,000 liters of alcohol per year
Water Source: Green Burn

The Green Burn is fed by springs that draw water from the Ben Rinnes Mountain. Before bubbling up as spring water and flowing into the Green Burn, water on the Ben Rinnes flows down the mountain slopes, passing heather and peat on its way to being absorbed underground and filtered through granite. Consequently, the spring water used for distillation is (according to Glenfarclas) "soft and slightly acidic, ideal for making whisky."

26. Glenfiddich

Pronunciation: glenFID-dik
Founded: 1887
Ownership: (since 1886) William Grant & Sons Ltd.
Capacity: 10,000,000 liters of alcohol per year
Water Source: Robbie Dubh Burn (also known as Robbie Dhu Burn)

Robbie Dubh Burn, a tributary of the River Fiddich, provides the distillery with soft, peaty, granite-filtered spring water, which is delivered through pipes to ensure that it doesn't get contaminated on its way from the Conval Hills (where the burn is located) to the distillery. The distillery's owner (William Grant & Sons) actually owns the 1,200 acres of land around the Robbie Dubh; this is so access to the burn can be limited, further ensuring that the distillery's water source will remain pure.

27. Glenglassaugh

Pronunciation: Glen-GLEAS-òch
Founded: 1875
Ownership: Glenglassaugh Distillery Company Ltd., owned by The Scaent Group

Capacity: 1,000,000 liters of alcohol per year
Water Source: Glassaugh Spring, Glassaugh River

The spring water from the Glassaugh Spring provides the distillery with high-quality water for distillation, while the Glassaugh River supplies the cooling water.

28. Glenlivet

Pronunciation: glen LIV-et
Founded: 1824
Ownership: (since 2001) Chivas Brothers, a subsidiary of Pernod Ricard
Capacity: 5,900,000 liters of alcohol per year
Water Source: Josie's Well

In Josie's Well springs naturally rock-filtered, mineral-rich, hard water that the Glenlivet distillery uses to meet its distillation needs.

29. Glenlossie

Pronunciation: glenLOSsie
Founded: 1876
Ownership: United Distillers and Vintners, a subsidiary of Diageo Plc

Capacity: 2,100,000 liters of alcohol per year
Water Source: Bardon Burn

Bardon Burn on Mannoch Hills supplies the distillery with clean water for distillation.

30. Glenrothes

Pronunciation: glenROTHes
Founded: 1878
Ownership: (since 1887) Highland Distillers, acquired by The Edrington Group
Capacity: 5,600,000 liters of alcohol per year
Water Source: Ardcanny Spring and Brauchhill Springs, Rothes Burn

Ardcanny and Brauchhill up in the Mannoch Hills supply the distillery with soft spring water for production. Rothes Burn provides the cooling water.

31. Glentauchers

Pronunciation: glen-TOCH-ers
Founded: 1898
Ownership: (since 2005) Chivas Brothers, a subsidiary of Pernod Ricard
Capacity: 3,400,000 liters of alcohol per year

Water Source: Rosarie Burn

The Rosarie Burn provides Glentauchers with the water it needs for distillation.

32. Inchgower

Pronunciation: INSJ-gower
Founded: 1871
Ownership: United Distillers and Vintners, a subsidiary of Diageo Plc
Capacity: Over 2,000,000 liters of alcohol per year
Water Source: Menduff Hills

Spring water rising in and flowing down the Menduff Hills provides Inchgower with clean water for distillation.

33. Kininvie

Pronunciation: kin-IN-view
Founded: 1992
Ownership: William Grant & Sons Ltd.
Capacity: 4,800,000 liters of alcoholper year
Water Source: Robbie Dubh Burn (also known as Robbie Dhu Spring)

Robbie Dubh Burn, a tributary of the River Fiddich, provides the distillery with soft, peaty, granite-filtered spring water, which is delivered through pipes to ensure that it doesn't get contaminated on its way from the Conval Hills (where the burn is located) to the distillery.

The distillery's owner (William Grant & Sons) actually owns the 1,200 acres of land around the Robbie Dubh; this is so access to the burn can be limited, further ensuring that the distillery's water source will remain pure.

Note: Kininvie is just a stillhouse. The feedstock that Kininvie distills into malt whisky is piped from the Balvenie distillery.

Kininvie bottles its malt whisky under the brands Kininvie and Hazelwood.

34. Knockando

Pronunciation: Nock-AN-doo
Founded: 1894
Ownership: United Distillers and Vintners, a subsidiary of Diageo Plc
Capacity: 1,290,000 liters of alcohol per year
Water Source: Cardnach Spring

In the hills above the distillery rises the Cardnach Spring, which supplies Knockando with exceptionally fresh spring water that has been naturally filtered through granite.

35. Knockdhu (anCnoc)

Pronunciation: Nok-DOO
Founded: 1898
Ownership: (since 1988) Inver House Distillers, a subsidiary of Pacific Spirit (U.K.) Ltd., now part of International Beverage Holdings Limited (InterBev)
Capacity: 1,000,000 liters of alcohol per year
Water Source: Knock Hill

Knockdhu draws its crystal-clear process water from several springs on the southern slopes of Knock Hill, the very hill after which the distillery's Single Malt Scotch Whisky is named.

Note: Knockdhu markets its Single Malt Scotch Whisky under the brand name, anCnoc. Meaning "black hill" in Scottish Gaelic, anCnoc is the local name for "Knock Hill"—the hill near the village of Knock where the Knockdhu distillery is located.

36. Linkwood

Pronunciation: LINKwood
Founded: 1821
Ownership: United Distillers and Vintners, a subsidiary of Diageo Plc
Capacity: 2,500,000 liters of alcohol per year
Water Source: Sources near Millbuies Loch

Linkwood gets its process water from the springs in the Loch Millbuies area, the very same springs that supply water to the Glen Elgin distillery.

37. Longmorn

Pronunciation: LONGmorn
Founded: 1894
Ownership: (since 1978) Chivas Brothers, a subsidiary of Pernod Ricard
Capacity: 3,500,000 liters of alcohol per year
Water Source: Boreholes on site

Longmorn, like its next-door neighbor the BenRiach distillery, uses spring water drawn through boreholes on site.

38. Macallan (The Macallan)

Pronunciation: Mac-ALLen
Founded: 1824
Ownership: (since 1996) Highland Distillers, acquired by The Edrington Group

Capacity: 6,000,000 liters of alcohol per year

Water Source: Borehole on site

Macallan has its own borehole from which it draws the spring water it uses for distillation.

Note: Macallan markets its whisky under the brand name, The Macallan. It is interesting to note that Macallan chooses to classify its single malts as "Highland Single Malt Scotch Whisky" instead of "Speyside Single Malt Scotch Whisky." Of course, this is legal. The region of Speyside is within the borders of the Highland region; thus, Speyside distilleries can call and label their Scotch whiskies as Highland Scotch whiskies if they want to do so.

39. MacDuff (Glen Deveron)

Pronunciation: mac-DUFF

Founded: 1962

Ownership: (since 1992) John Dewar & Sons Ltd., a subsidiary of Bacardi Ltd.

Capacity: 2,400,000 liters of alcohol per year

Water Source: Gelly Burn, River Deveron

The distillery's process water comes from Gelly Burn, while the cooling water comes from its namesake, the River Deveron.

Note: MacDuff bottles its whisky under the "Glen Deveron" brand name, while independent bottlers bottle whisky from Macduff under the "Macduff" brand name. Additionally, Macduff uses the "Highland" instead of the "Speyside" regional classification.

40. Mannochmore

Pronunciation: mannock-MORE

Founded: 1972

Ownership: United Distillers and Vintners, a subsidiary of Diageo Plc

Capacity: 3,200,000 liters of alcohol per year

Water Source: Bardon Burn

Bardon Burn on Mannoch Hills supplies the distillery with clean water for distillation.

41. Miltonduff

Pronunciation: Mil-ten-DUFF

Founded: 1824

Ownership: (since 2005) Chivas Brothers, a subsidiary of Pernod Ricard

Capacity: 5,500,000 liters of alcohol per year
Water Source: Black Burn

The Black Burn flows past the Miltonduff on its way to the River Lossie and provides the distillery with clean spring water from the Romach Hills.

Note: From 1964 to 1981, the Miltonduff distillery also produced an expression of Single Malt Scotch known as the "Mosstowie." However, Miltonduff did not release official bottlings of this malt.

42. Mortlach

Pronunciation: MORT-lack
Founded: 1823
Ownership: United Distillers and Vintners, a subsidiary of Diageo Plc
Capacity: 2,900,000 liters of alcohol per year
Water Source: Conval Hills, River Dullan

Mortlach sources its process water from springs in the Conval Hills. A tributary of the River Fiddich, River Dullan, provides the distillery with cooling water.

43. Roseisle

Pronunciation: rose-isle
Founded: 2010 (officially opened as a distillery; has been a malting facility for Diageo since 1979)
Ownership: Diageo Plc
Capacity: 10,000,000 liters of alcohol per year
Water Source: Boreholes on site

Roseisle has its own underground water source. This underground water is rather murky and contains higher than desirable levels of iron and manganese. Thus, Roseisle built its own water treatment facility to prepare its water for process use.

Roseisle also recycles its own water. However, it uses recycled water only for barley processing/malting, not the actual distillation.

Note: Roseisle will mainly produce malt whisky for Diageo's blends, but its malt whisky will also be bottled as a single malt.

44. Speyburn

Pronunciation: s-PAY-burn
Founded: 1897

Ownership: (since 1991) Inver House Distillers, a subsidiary of Pacific Spirit (U.K.) Ltd., now part of International Beverage Holdings Limited (InterBev)
Capacity: 2,000,000 liters of alcohol per year
Water Source: Granty Burn

A tributary of the River Spey, Granty Burn provides Speyburn with soft, clear spring water for distillation. Water from this source is piped from approximately a mile away.

45. Speyside

Pronunciation: Speyside
Founded: 1990
Ownership: Speyside Distillers Co Ltd.
Capacity: 500,000 liters of alcohol per year
Water Source: Tromie River

This tributary of River Spey supplies the distillery with both process and cooling water. Water from River Tromie is drawn to the distillery through an old mill lade.

Note: The Speyside Distillery produces various expressions of malt whisky and uses/has used the following brands on their official bottlings: Speyside, Great Glen, Glentromie, Drumguish, and Cú Dhub.

46. Strathisla

Pronunciation: Strath-EYE-la
Founded: 1786
Ownership: (since 1950) Chivas Brothers, a subsidiary of Pernod Ricard
Capacity: 2,400,000 liters of alcohol per year
Water Source: Fons Bulliens

The spring water from the well of Fons Bulliens is non-peaty and slightly hard (due to its calcium content).

Note: Strathisla used to be known as Milltown.

47. Strathmill

Pronunciation: strath-MILL
Founded: 1891
Ownership: United Distillers and Vintners, a subsidiary of Diageo Plc
Capacity: 1,700,000 liters of alcohol per year
Water Source: Spring on site, River Isla

There is a spring on site that supplies the distillery with

fresh water for distillation. For cooling, the distillery draws water from the River Isla.

48. Tamdhu

Pronunciation: TAM-doo
Founded: 1896
Ownership: (since 2011) Ian Macleod Distillers Ltd.
Capacity: 4,500,000 liters of alcohol per year
Water Source: Local spring, Knockando Burn

A local spring provides the distillery with fresh and excellent process water, while the Knockando Burn nearby provides the cooling water.

49. Tamnavulin

Pronunciation: TAM-na-VOO-lin
Founded: 1966
Ownership: (since 1993) Whyte & Mackay, a subsidiary of United Spirits Ltd.
Capacity: 4,000,000 liters of alcohol per year
Water Source: Easterton Springs

Springs in Easterton feed an underground reservoir on site, and it is from this reservoir that Tamnavulin takes its process water.

50. Tomintoul

Pronunciation: TOM-in-TOWL
Founded: 1965
Ownership: (since 2000) Angus Dundee Distillers Plc
Capacity: 3,000,000 liters of alcohol per year
Water Source: Ballantruan Spring

This water source in the Cromdale Hills gives the Tomintoul distillery a steady supply of fresh spring water for distillation.

51. Tormore

Pronunciation: torMORE
Founded: 1960
Ownership: (since 2005) Chivas Brothers, a subsidiary of Pernod Ricard
Capacity: 3,700,000 liters of alcohol per year
Water Source: Achvochkie Burn

This water source is fed by springs in the Craggan More.

ISLAY

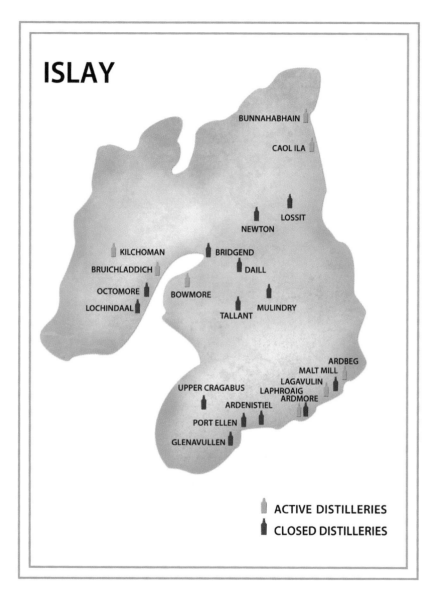

BUNNAHABHAIN

CAOL ILA

LOSSIT

NEWTON

KILCHOMAN

BRIDGEND

BRUICHLADDICH

DAILL

OCTOMORE

BOWMORE

LOCHINDAAL

MULINDRY

TALLANT

ARDBEG

MALT MILL

LAGAVULIN

UPPER CRAGABUS

LAPHROAIG

ARDMORE

ARDENISTIEL

PORT ELLEN

GLENAVULLEN

ACTIVE DISTILLERIES

CLOSED DISTILLERIES

ISLAY

The protected whisky locality of Islay has eight active distilleries that produce a combined total of around 15,650,000 liters of Scotch per year. Caol Ila, which has a production capacity of 3,600,000 liters, accounts for 23% of this protected whisky locality's annual production.

1. Ardbeg

Pronunciation: ard-BEG
Founded: 1815
Ownership: (since 1997) The Glenmorangie Company, a subsidiary of Moët Hennessy - Louis Vuitton
Capacity: 1,000,000 liters of alcohol per year
Water Source: Loch Uigeadail

Loch Uigeadail, which is approximately 3 miles away from Ardbeg, is located on the hill behind the distillery. The fresh water from this source rises through quartzite and flows over peat bogs; it travels down the hill, meets the Airgh Nam Beist (Shelter of the Beast)—another lake—then proceeds to supply water to Charlie's Dam, from which Ardbeg gets its soft process water.

2. Bowmore

Pronunciation: bow-MORE
Founded: 1779

Ownership: Morrison Bowmore Distillers, a subsidiary of Suntory
Capacity: 2,000,000 liters of alcohol per year
Water Source: Laggan River

A lade around nine miles long brings water from a source on River Laggan to Bowmore. Bowmore's process water is dark and peaty since the River Laggan passes over peat bogs (and flows through rushes, ferns, and moss) as it runs its course toward the lade that diverts some of its water to Bowmore.

3. Bruichladdich

Pronunciation: brookLADdie
Founded: 1881
Ownership: Bruichladdich Distillery Co. Ltd., which is now (specifically, since July 2012) owned by Rémy Cointreau UK Ltd[3]
Capacity: 1,500,000 liters of alcohol per year
Water Source: Bruichladdich Loch, Dirty Dotty's Spring, Bruichladdich Burn

---

[3] This is according to Bruichladdich (http://www.bruichladdich.com/news/laddie-news/bruichladdich-remy-cointreau-agreement), accessed on October 31, 2013.

The distillery pipes mashing water directly from the Bruichladdich Loch, which is two miles above the distillery. The brown water of this lake comes from beneath the bedrock, passing through peat then clay before emerging—thoroughly softened and cleansed—to the surface.

Dirty Dotty's Spring (which is on Octomore Farm and is approximately two miles away from Bruichladdich) provides the distillery with the clear spring water it uses to cut its sprit from cask strength to bottling strength. Bruichladdich Burn nearby provides the cooling water.

4. Bunnahabhain

Pronunciation: boona-HAAven
Founded: 1883
Ownership: (since 2003) Burn Stewart Distillers Ltd., now part of Distell
Capacity: 2,500,000 liters of alcohol per year
Water Source: Margadale Spring, Abhainn Araig

Water from the Margadale Spring (the spring is located at Margadale, thus its name) is piped down to the distillery and used as process water, while water from Abhainn Araig serves as the distillery's cooling water.

5. Caol Ila

Pronunciation: cull-EEla
Founded: 1846
Ownership: United Distillers and Vintners, a subsidiary of Diageo Plc
Capacity: 3,600,000 liters of alcohol per year
Water Source: Loch nam Ban

Percolating through limestone, the spring water of Loch nam Ban (which is located in the hill above Caol Ila) is slightly hard. It is peaty, as is typical of water in Islay; however, it does tend to be less peaty than water from other sources in the island.

6. Kilchoman

Pronunciation: kilHOman
Founded: 2005

Ownership: Kilchoman Distillery Co. Ltd.
Capacity: 100,000 liters of alcohol per year
Water Source: Local source

A spring rising in the hills just behind the Bruichladdich distillery is the source of process water for Kilchoman. Water from this source obtains its distinct character from the peat and moss over which it flows as it runs its course.

7. Lagavulin

Pronunciation: LAG-a-VOO-lin
Founded: 1816
Ownership: United Distillers and Vintners, a subsidiary of Diageo Plc
Capacity: 2,250,000 liters of alcohol per year
Water Source: Lochs on Solan Hill

The lakes in Solan Hill, which is located behind the distillery, feed the fast-flowing, peat-brown stream that supplies process water to Lagavulin. This stream flows over moss and peat deposits on its course toward the distillery, and this accounts for the water's unique character.

8. Laphroaig

Pronunciation: La-FROYG
Founded: 1815
Ownership: Beam Global, owned by Fortune Brands
Capacity: 2,700,000 liters of alcohol per year
Water Source: Kilbride Stream / Kilbride River

Laphroaig built a dam or reservoir on the Kilbride Stream (otherwise known as the Kilbride River) to make sure the distillery has a steady and ready supply of water from this source. To protect its water rights, Laphroaig bought the land around the stream.

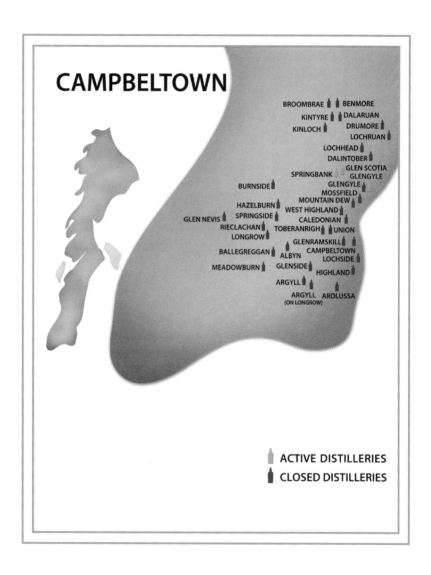

CAMPBELTOWN

BROOMBRAE · BENMORE
KINTYRE · DALARUAN
KINLOCH · DRUMORE
LOCHRUAN
LOCHHEAD
DALINTOBER
GLEN SCOTIA
SPRINGBANK · GLENGYLE
BURNSIDE · GLENGYLE
MOSSFIELD
MOUNTAIN DEW
HAZELBURN · WEST HIGHLAND
GLEN NEVIS · SPRINGSIDE · CALEDONIAN
RIECLACHAN · TOBERANRIGH · UNION
LONGROW
GLENRAMSKILL
BALLEGREGGAN · CAMPBELTOWN
ALBYN · LOCHSIDE
MEADOWBURN · GLENSIDE
HIGHLAND
ARGYLL
ARGYLL · ARDLUSSA
(ON LONGROW)

ACTIVE DISTILLERIES
CLOSED DISTILLERIES

CAMPBELTOWN

There are only three actively operating distilleries in the protected whisky locality of Campbeltown. These distilleries produce a total of 3,500,000 liters of whisky every year.

1. Glen Scotia

Pronunciation: glen SCOH-sja
Founded: 1832
Ownership: (since 1999) Loch Lomond Distillery Company Ltd.
Capacity: 750,000 liters of alcohol per year
Water Source: Crosshill Loch

Regularly replenished by Campbeltown's summer rains, Crosshill Loch provides the distillery with soft, peaty, brownish process water.

2. Springbank

Pronunciation: spring-BANK
Founded: 1828
Ownership: (since 1989) Springbank Distillers Ltd., a subsidiary of J&A Mitchell & Co Ltd.
Capacity: 2,000,000 liters of alcohol per year
Water Source: Crosshill Loch

Crosshill Loch also supplies process water to Glen Scotia and Glengyle. See Glen Scotia distillery above for more information on the water of Crosshill Loch.

Note: The Springbank Distillery makes three brands of Campbeltown Single Malt Scotch Whisky: Springbank, Longrow, and Hazelburn.

3. Glengyle (Kilkerran)

Founded: 2000 (officially opened in 2004)
Ownership: Mitchell's Glengyle Ltd., a subsidiary of J&A Mitchell & Co. Ltd.
Capacity: 750,000 liters of alcohol per year
Water Source: Crosshill Loch

Crosshill Loch also supplies process water to Glen Scotia and Springbank. See Glen Scotia distillery above for more information on the water of Crosshill Loch.

Note: Glengyle bottles its Single Malt Scotch Whisky under the "Kilkerran" brand, not the "Glengyle" brand since the latter is already in use as the name of a blended whisky.

This distillery filled its first six casks in 2004, originally intending to age this batch for 12 years; it should have released its first bottling only in 2016. In 2009, however, Glengyle released 12,000 bottles of its 5-year old single malt, and the distillery has continued releasing yearly bottlings ever since. This is part of the distillery's "Work in Progress" series, which ought to let fans of the brand track Kilkerran Single Malt's development from the 5-year-old to the mature 12-year-old it will become in 2016.

LIST OF CLOSED DISTILLERIES

Below is a list of closed distilleries that used to produce Single Malt Scotch Whisky. As with the list of active distilleries above, the closed distilleries are organized by region.

Note: The following list focuses on closed distilleries believed to have made malt whisky. Even distilleries that could not be confirmed to have sold or bottled single malt expressions are included; independent bottlers could have still obtained casks and sold them as Single Malt Scotch.

Caveat: There's usually little to no record of closed distilleries, especially the really old ones. This means that the following list might not be exhaustive;

Single Malt Scotch production might also have been erroneously attributed to some distilleries. Furthermore, ownership information *usually* pertains to the last known owner.

HIGHLAND

There are 38 closed malt distilleries on record in the Highland Region: 13 in the East, 13 in the North, 8 in the South, and 4 in the West.

Closed EAST HIGHLANDS Distilleries

1. Auchinblae

Founded: 1896

Closed: 1930

Ownership: Distillers Company Ltd., which became part of United Distillers and Vintners, a subsidiary of Diageo Plc

Water Source: a spring at Templebank

2. Benachie / Bennachie

Founded: 1824

Closed: 1913

Ownership: Lawrence Mac-Donald Chalmers

Water Source: Jordan Burn

Note: This was founded as the Jericho Distillery but was later renamed Benachie. While the distillery is closed, the name "Bennachie" continues to be a brand of vatted or blended malt whisky.

3. Corgarff Castle Distillery

Founded: 1826

Closed: Unknown; probably 1831 when the soldiers garrisoned at Corgarff Castle left.

Ownership: James McHardy

Note: This licensed distillery was burned down on July 17, 1826—the same year it was established. Apparently, legal distillation at that time was considered a betrayal by illegal whisky distillers, who did everything they could—say, assaulting legal distillers and even burning down licensed distilleries—so legal distillation would stop. James McHar-dy, who was one of the illegal distillers of whisky before he set up a licensed distillery in Corgarff Castle, was not exempt from the threat posed by illegal smugglers, and his distillery at Corgarff Castle was subsequently burned to the ground.

4. Gilcomston

Founded: 1751

Closed: 1763

Ownership: Thomson, Elsmie & Co.

5. Glenaden

Founded: 1845

Closed: 1915

Ownership: T. Yelton Ogilvie

Water Source: Biffie Springs

6. Glencoull

Founded: 1897

Closed: 1929

Ownership: George Duncan

7. Glenesk[4]

Pronunciation: glen-ESK
Founded: 1897
Closed: 1985
Ownership: William Sanderson & Sons Ltd. (but Glenesk was acquired by Greencore Maltings Group in 1997)
Water Source: North Esk River

Note: This distillery has borne different names since its founding. It was established as Highland Esk, but it was later changed to North Esk, then to Montrose, then to Hillside, before it was finally called the Glenesk five years before it closed.

8. Glenugie[5]

Pronunciation: Glen YOU-gee
Founded: 1831

Closed: 1983
Ownership: Whitbread and Co.

Note: Between 1831 and 1983 were long periods in which the distillery did not operate or was actually closed.

9. Glenury Royal[6]

Pronunciation:
Glen-YOU-ree Royal
Founded: 1825
Closed: 1985
Ownership: John Gillon & Co.

10. Lochside[7]

Pronunciation: LOCH-side
Founded: 1957
Closed: 1992

---

[4]Definitely a single malt whisky distillery. Master of Malt (http://www.masterofmalt.com/whiskies/glen-esk-1984-whisky/) has a listing for a Gordon and MacPhail bottling of a 1984 distillation, 20-year-old Glen Esk Single Malt Scotch Whisky.

[5]Definitely a single malt whisky distillery. Master of Malt (http://www.masterofmalt.com/distilleries/glenugie-whisky-distillery/) has listings for an official bottling and independent bottlings of Glenugie Single Malt Scotch Whisky.

[6]Definitely a single malt whisky distillery. Master of Malt (http://www.masterofmalt.com/distilleries/glenury-whisky-distillery/) has listings for official and independent bottlings of Glenury Royal Single Malt Scotch Whisky.

[7]Definitely a single malt whisky. Master of Malt (http://www.masterofmalt.com/distilleries/lochside-whisky-distillery/) has listings for independent bottlings of this highland distillery's Single Malt Scotch Whisky.

Ownership: Destilerias y Crianza del Whisky SA of Madrid, a subsidiary of Pedro Domecq Sherry

Water Source: Boreholes on site

11. Millfield

Founded: 1798

Closed: Unknown

Ownership: John Cumine

12. North Port / Brechin[8]

Founded: 1820

Closed: 1983

Ownership: Distillers Company Ltd., which became part of United Distillers and Vintners, a subsidiary of Diageo Plc

Water Source: Loch Lee

13. Strathdee

Founded: 1821

Closed: 1941

Ownership: Associated Scottish Distilleries Ltd., a subsidiary of Train & McIntyre Ltd., owned by National Distillers of America

Water Source: Manofield Burn as well as the city mains

Closed NORTH HIGHLANDS Distilleries

1. Banff[9]

Pronunciation: banf or bampf

Founded: 1824

Closed: 1983

Ownership: Distillers Company Ltd., which became part of United Distillers and Vintners, a subsidiary of Diageo Plc

2. Ben Morven

Founded: 1886

Closed: 1911

Ownership: Northern Distilleries Ltd.

---

[8]Definitely a single malt whisky distillery. Master of Malt (http://www.masterofmalt.com/distilleries/north-port-whisky-distillery/) has listings for North Port Single Malt Scotch Whisky bottlings by Diageo and independent bottlers.

[9]Definitely a single malt whisky. At Master of Malt (http://www.masterofmalt.com/distilleries/banff-whisky-distillery/), there are listings for old and rare Banff Single Malt Scotch Whisky from independent bottlers as well as from Diageo.

Water Source: Calder Burn

Note: When first established, this was named after the closed Gerston distillery, so it was known as Gerston II. It was later renamed Ben Morven.

3. Ben Wyvis[10]

Founded: 1965

Closed: 1976

Ownership: Whyte & Mackay Ltd.

Note: This Ben Wyvis distillery was named after—but does not refer to—the original Ben Wyvis distillery, also closed, which operated from 1879 to 1926.

4. Ben Wyvis / Ferintosh

Founded: 1879

Closed: 1926

Ownership: Ferintosh Distillery Co. Ltd.

Note: Renamed Ferintosh in 1893, this was the original Ben Wyvis Distillery—the one that stood near Dingwall, not the one in Invergordon.

5. Brora[11]

Pronunciation: BRO-ra

Founded: 1819

Closed: 1983

Ownership: Scottish Malt Distillers, a subsidiary of Distillers Company Ltd., which became part of United Distillers and Vintners, a subsidiary of Diageo Plc

Water Source: Clynemilton Burn

---

[10]Definitely a single malt whisky distillery. Master of Malt (http://www.masterofmalt.com/whiskies/ben-wyvis-1965-37-year-old-whisky/) carries a listing for a 37-year-old Ben Wyvis Single Malt Scotch Whisky, valued at a staggering £1,114.99.

[11]Definitely a single malt whisky distillery. Master of Malt (http://www.masterofmalt.com/distilleries/brora-whisky-distillery/) carries listings for Brora Single Malt Scotch Whisky. This was originally established as the Clynelish distillery, but it was changed to Brora in 1969. The other Clynelish distillery, built in 1967 on the adjacent lot, retained the Clynelish name.

6. Ferintosh

Founded: 1690

Closed: 1784 (supposedly, distillation in Ferintosh—through 29 licensed stills—resumed around 1792)

Ownership: Duncan Forbes

Note: It is not explicitly stated that the distillery was closed in 1784, only that the Forbes family's duty-free distillation privileges were withdrawn. Ferintosh was simply the name by which Forbes' distilleries—and consequently Forbes' whisky—in Ferintosh were known. In actuality, it was made up of individual distilleries including the ones in Ryefield, Gallow Hill, and Mulchaich.

7. Geise

Founded: 1851

Closed: 1852

Ownership: Unknown

8. Gerston

Founded: 1796

Closed: 1875

Ownership: James C. Swanson

Water Source: Calder Burn, which is fed by Loch Calder

9. Glen Albyn[12]

Pronunciation: Glen AOL-bin

Founded: 1846

Closed: 1983

Ownership: Distillers Company Ltd., which became part of United Distillers and Vintners, a subsidiary of Diageo Plc

Water Source: Loch Ness

10. Glen Mhor[13]

Pronunciation: Glen VHOR

Founded: 1892

Closed: 1983

Ownership: Distillers Company

[12]Definitely a single malt whisky distillery. At Master of Malt (http://www.masterofmalt.com/whiskies/glen-albyn-1981-signatory-bottling-whisky/), there's a listing for a Signatory bottling of a rare 28-year-old Single Single Malt Scotch Whisky, distilled in 1981 by Glen Albyn.

[13]Definitely a single malt whisky distillery. At Master of Malt (http://www.masterofmalt.com/distilleries/glen-mhor-whisky-distillery/), there are several listings for Glen Mhor Single Malt Scotch Whisky bottlings from independent bottlers, from Glen Mhor and from Diageo.

Ltd., which became part of United Distillers and Vintners, a subsidiary of Diageo Plc

Water Source: Loch Ness

11. Glenskiach[14]

Founded: 1896

Closed: In 1932 the final meeting about winding up the distillery was held. However, the distillery had stopped producing by 1926. The distillery was demolished in 1933.

Ownership: Glenskiach Distillery Company Ltd.

Water Source: Skiach

12. Millburn[15]

Pronunciation: millBURN

Founded: 1805

Closed: 1985

Ownership: Distillers Company Ltd., which became part of United Distillers and Vintners, a subsidiary of Diageo Plc

Water Source: Loch Duntelchaig

13. Milltown

Founded: 1817

Closed: Unknown

Ownership: Alexander Ross

Closed SOUTH HIGHLANDS Distilleries

1. Auchnagie

Founded: 1812

Closed: 1912

Ownership: John Dewar & Sons Ltd.

Water Source: Auchnagie Hills

2. Ballechin

Founded: 1810

Closed: 1927

Ownership: William Rose

3. Easterkepp

Founded: 1825

Closed: 1842

Ownership: John Cassells

---

[14]Evidence indicates that this produced Single Malt Scotch. At Whiskypedia (http://singlemaltwhiskyminis.strefa.pl/others-32.html), the owner of the site—a collector of Single Malt Scotch Whisky mini bottles—shows a picture of a mini-bottle of a Glenskiach Single Malt Scotch (independent bottling).

[15]Definitely a single malt whisky distillery. A 17-year-old Single Malt Scotch Whisky, distilled in 1971, is currently (February 1, 2013) for sale at http://www.thewhiskyexchange.com/B-40-Millburn.aspx for a whopping £350.00.

Note: This distillery was "founded" when the Kepp distillery was split into two distilleries: the Easterkepp and the Westerkepp.

was simply divided into two distilleries—the Easterkepp and the Westerkepp (with the latter becoming the Glenfoyle distillery.

4. Glenturret

Founded: 1814

Closed: 1852

Ownership: William Philips & Son

Note: This was the original Glenturret distillery. It was known by names such as Glenfinch and Hoshmill until 1826, when it was called Glenturret.

5. Kepp

Founded: 1795

Closed: 1825

Ownership: David Cassells, followed by his son, John Cassells

Note: Strictly speaking, the distillery was not closed in 1825; it

6. Stronachie[16]

Founded: 1890s

Closed: 1928

Ownership: St. James Export Co. Ltd.

Water Source: Chapel Burn

7. Tomdachoill

Founded: 1816

Closed: 1878

Ownership: John Duff (when it closed, but the site is now owned by Ian Buxton)

8. Westerkepp / Glenfoyle

Founded: 1825

Closed: 1923

---

[16]Most likely a single malt whisky distillery. Today, A.D.Rattray bottles a "Stronachie 12-year-old" and a "Stronachie 18-year-old," but these are **not** distilled by the now-defunct Stronachie but by Benrinnes. However, based on the information released by A.D. Rattray (http://www.whiskyintelligence.com/2010/07/stronachie-%E2%80%93-lost-in-time-not-in-spirit%E2%80%A6-scotch-whisky-news/) , it appears that the flavor profile of the present-day Stronachie whisky was determined by matching it as closely as possible to that of the original Stronachie 1904-distilled whisky, of which only four bottles remain.

Ownership: John Dewar & Sons (when it closed but Invergordon Distillers owned the site until 1971)

Water Source: Campsie Fells

Note: This distillery was "founded" when the Kepp distillery was split into two distilleries: the Easterkepp and the Westerkepp. It was later renamed Glenfoyle.

Closed WEST HIGHLANDS DISTILLERIES

1. Glenlochy[17]

Pronunciation: Glen LOCK-key

Founded: 1898

Closed: 1983

Ownership: Scottish Malt Distillers, a subsidiary of Distillers Company Ltd., which became part of United Distillers and Vintners, a subsidiary of Diageo Plc

2. Lochgilphead

Founded: 1816

Closed: Unknown

Ownership: William Hay & Co.

3. Nevis

Founded: 1878

Closed: 1908

Ownership: Donald McDonald

Water Source: Buchan's Well

Note: The Nevis distillery was supposedly joined with the Ben Nevis distillery, which preceded it.

4. Glenfyne / Glengilp / Glendarroch[18]

Founded: 1831

Closed: 1937

Ownership: Glenfyne Distillery Co. Ltd.

Water Source: Ard Burn

---

[17]Definitely a single malt whisky distillery. Master of Malt (http://www.masterofmalt.com/distilleries/glenlochy-whisky-distillery/) has listings of Glenlochy Single Malt Scotch Whisky bottled by independent bottlers.

[18]Definitely a single malt whisky distillery. Glenfyne produced single malt whisky under the brand name Glamis, and, according to Luxist (http://www.luxist.com/2010/10/27/glenfyne-single-malt-expected-to-fetch-10-000/), a 10-year-old Glamis Single Malt Scotch Whisky from Glenfyne was expected to fetch £10,000 at the Bonhams' Whisky Sale in November 2010.

ISLANDS

There are two closed Island malt distilleries on record.

1. Corry

Founded: 1816

Closed: 1826

Ownership: Lachlan McKinnon

Location: Broadford, Isle of Skye

2. Stornoway

Founded: 1825

Closed: 1840

Ownership: Stornoway Distillery Co.

Location: Stornoway, Isle of Lewis

LOWLAND

There are 45 closed Lowland malt distilleries on record.

1. Abbeyhill / Croftanrigh

Founded: Unknown

Closed: 1852

Ownership: J.A. Bernard

Note: The original Abbeyhill distillery was closed in 1826 when the owner, Thomas Miller, went bankrupt. In 1846, a new distillery rose in its place; it was called the Croftanrigh.

2. Auchtermuchty / Stratheden

Founded: 1829

Closed: 1926

Ownership: G. & W. Bonthrone

3. Auchtertool

Founded: 1845

Closed: 1927

Ownership: Distillers Company Ltd., which became part of United Distillers and Vintners, a subsidiary of Diageo Plc

4. Avonglen

Founded: Unknown

Closed: 1830

Ownership: John Burns & Co.

5. Bank

Founded: 1825

Closed: 1937

Ownership: John Findlay

6. Bonnington / Leith

Founded: 1798

Closed: 1853

Ownership: Balenie & Kemp

7. Bonnytown / Bonnyton

Founded: 1795

Closed: 1826

Ownership: More & Williamson

8. Cambus

Founded: 1806

Closed: 1993

Ownership: United Malt & Grain Distillers Ltd.

Note: It was converted to a grain distillery in 1836,[19] but before that, it might have produced malt whisky without ever making an official release of single malt whisky.

9. Canonmills

Founded: 1782

Closed: 1970s

Ownership: J. Haig & Sons

10. Carsebridge

Founded: 1799

Closed: 1983

Ownership: Scottish Grain Distillers, Ltd.

Note: Established as a malt distillery, it was converted to a grain distillery only in the early 1850s.[20] It is more than possible that it made single malt whisky—although perhaps the distillery did not sell the malt whisky it made.

11. Cowie

Founded: Unknown

Closed: 1860

Ownership: James McNab

---

[19]Worm Tub (n.d.) Cambus Distillery. Date accessed: February 11, 2013 (http://www.wormtub.com/distilleries/distillery.php?distillery=Cambus).

[20]Scotland Whisky and Distilleries. (n.d.). Carsbridge. Date accessed: February 11, 2013 (http://www.whisky-distilleries.info/Distilleries/Carsebridge_EN.shtml).

12. Dean

Founded: 1881

Closed: 1922

Ownership: Scottish Malt Distillers Ltd., a subsidiary of Distillers Company Ltd., which became part of United Distillers and Vintners, a subsidiary of Diageo Plc.

13. Drumcaldie

Founded: 1896

Closed: 1903

Ownership: Distillers Company Ltd., which became part of United Distillers and Vintners, a subsidiary of Diageo Plc

14. Dundashill[21]

Founded: 1770

Closed: 1902

Ownership: Distillers Company Ltd., which became part of United Distillers and Vintners, a subsidiary of Diageo Plc

15. Edinburgh

Founded: 1849

Closed: 1925

Ownership: Scottish Malt Distillers Ltd., a subsidiary of Distillers Company Ltd., which became part of United Distillers and Vintners, a subsidiary of Diageo Plc

Water Source: Pentland Hills

Note: This distillery was founded under the name West Sciennes. It was thereafter renamed as Newington then Glen Sciennes until 1859, when it was called Edinburgh.

16. Finnieston

Founded: 1824

Closed: 1827

Ownership: Ebenezer Connal

17. Glen Newton

Founded: Unknown

Closed: 1855

Ownership: Alexander Duncan

---

[21]Definitely a single malt whisky distillery. According to Ulf Buxrud's Lost Distilleries 1885-1945 (retrieved on February 9, 2013, from http://www.buxrud.se/lost.htm), this distillery made and sold single malt whisky.

18. Glenforth

Founded: 1843

Closed: 1867

Ownership: John Stewart & Co

19. Glenmavis[22]

Founded: 1795

Closed: 1910

Ownership: John MacNab

20. Glenochil

Founded: 1746

Closed: 1929

Ownership: Distillers Company Ltd., which became part of United Distillers and Vintners, a subsidiary of Diageo Plc

Water Source: Balquhan Burns

21. Glenpatrick / Gleniffer

Founded: 1833

Closed: 1894

Ownership: Glenpatrick Distillery Co.

Water Source: Gleniffer Burn

22. Glentarras

Founded: 1839

Closed: 1914

Ownership: Glentarras Distillery Co.

Water Source: Gaulsike Burn

23. Grange

Founded: Unknown

Closed: 1851

Ownership: John Philp & Co. (when it closed)

24. Grange Distillery Burntisland / The Grange[23]

Founded: 1786

Closed: 1927

Ownership: Scottish Malt Distillers Ltd., a subsidiary of Dis-

---

[22]Definitely a single malt whisky distillery. According to Ulf Buxrud's Lost Distilleries 1885-1945 (retrieved on February 9, 2013, from http://www.buxrud.se/lost.htm), this distillery produced single malt whisky and, in 1855, started producing single malt whisky using a Coffey still. Incidentally, that Coffey-still malt whisky Glenmavis produced after 1855 would not qualify as Single Malt Scotch today; modern regulations say Single Malt Scotch must be distilled using pot stills.

[23]Definitely a single malt whisky distillery. Burntisland.net (http://www.burntisland. net/distillery.htm, accessed on February 10, 2013) shows bottle labels indicating that the distillery bottled whisky from "pure malt" and makes a reference to an official bottling of Grange malt that sold for more than £2,000.

tillers Company Ltd., which became part of United Distillers and Vintners, a subsidiary of Diageo Plc

Water Source: Binn Burn and Lonsdale Burn (fed by the Binn Burn) then later piped directly from Dunearn Loch that supplied the Binn Burn

25. Haddington (of Nungate)

Founded: Unknown

Closed: Unknown

Ownership: James Cumming

26. Haddington (of Westfield)

Founded: Unknown

Closed: Unknown

Ownership: John Crabbie & Co.

27. Hattonburn

Founded: 1780

Closed: Unknown

Ownership: Andrew and Charles Stein

28. Inverleven[24]

Founded: 1938

Closed: 1991

Ownership: Chivas Brothers, a subsidiary of Pernod Ricard

Water Source: Loch Lomond

Note: This distillery was classified as "closed" rather than "deactivated" because its distilling equipment had already been transported to Islay to be used in the planned reopening of the Lochindaal distillery—this time as the Port Ellen distillery.[25]

29. Kennetpans

Founded: before 1730s; Kennetpans was supposedly the largest distillery in Scotland by the 1730s

Closed: 1825

Ownership: John Stein

[24]Definitely a single malt whisky distillery. Master of Malt (http://www.masterofmalt.com/distilleries/inverleven-whisky-distillery/, accessed February 10, 2013) has listings for independent bottlings of Inverleven Single Malt Scotch Whisky.

[25]This is according to Islay Info (http://www.islayinfo.com/islay_port_charlotte_distillery.html, accessed on February 10, 2013).

30. Kinclaith[26]

Pronunciation: Kin-KLATHE
Founded: 1957
Closed: 1975
Ownership: Whitbread & Co. Ltd.
Water Source: Loch Katrine

31. Kirkliston

Founded: 1795
Closed: 1920

Ownership: Stewart & Co., one of the founders of Distillers Company Ltd., which became part of United Distillers and Vintners, a subsidiary of Diageo Plc

Water Source: The burns of Craigmaiellen and Humbie

32. Ladyburn

Founded: 1966

Closed: 1975 (demolished in 1976)

Ownership: William Grant & Sons Ltd.

Water Source: (could have been) Penwhapple Reservoir

This distillery, on which site now stands the Ailsa Bay malt distillery (also by William Grant & Sons Ltd.), probably used water from the same source that supposedly supplies Ailsa Bay - the Penwhapple Reservoir.

Ladyburn was definitely a Single Malt Scotch distillery. It released single malt expressions under the "Ladyburn" brand, while independent bottlers bottled Ladyburn single malt under the Ayrshire brand.

33. Langholm

Founded: 1765
Closed: 1917
Ownership: Langholm Distillery Co.

34. Lasswade

Founded: Unknown
Closed: Unknown
Ownership: John McNab & Co.

---

[26]Definitely a single malt whisky distillery, although it existed within a grain distillery complex and never officially bottled its single malt whisky. Even so, Kinclaith Single Malt Scotch Whisky is available from independent bottlers as this listing from Master of Malt shows (http://www.masterofmalt.com/distilleries/kinclaith-whisky-distillery/, accessed on February 10, 2013)

35. Litlemill[27]

Brands: Dumbuck, Dunglass and Littlemill

Founded: 1772

Closed: 1994 (when production ceased), in 2006 it was demolished

Ownership: Loch Lomond Distillery Co. Ltd.

Water Source: Kilpatrick Springs

Note: Littlemill single malt whisky releases usually come under the Littlemill brand name, but Littlemill made special malts and released them under different names: the Dumbuck and the Dunglass. The Dumbuck was a heavily peated single malt, while the Dunglass was a completely unpeated single malt.

36. Mains

Founded: Unknown

Closed: Unknown

Ownership: James Glen

37. Moffat[28]

Brands: Glen Flagler, Killyloch (or Lillyloch) and Islebrae

Founded: 1965 when production began

Closed: Glen Flagler closed in 1985, Killyloch and Islebrae closed in 1970

Ownership: Invergordon Distillers

Water Source: Lilly Loch

Note: Moffat was the name of the distillery complex. It had a grain distillery, but it also had two malt lines that produced Single Malt Scotch Whisky. The primary malt line produced Glen Flagler Single Malt Scotch Whisky, which was a pot-still single malt until 1969, when the line produced wash using a continuous still. The secondary malt line produced Killyloch single malt whisky, which was meant mainly for blending but casks of which some independent bottlers were able to obtain; this secondary line also produced Islebrae.

---

[27]Definitely a single malt whisky distillery. Master of Malt (http://www.masterofmalt.com/distilleries/littlemill-whisky-distillery/, accessed on February 9, 2013) has listings for independent bottlings of single malt whisky from Littlemill.

[28]Definitely a single malt whisky distillery. According to Ulf Buxrud (http://www.buxrud.se/samling.htm, retrieved on February 9, 2013), the Moffat distillery's primary malt line produced pot-still Glen Flagler single malt whisky until 1969, the year when it started producing wash using a continuous still.

38. Old Rome

Founded: Unknown

Closed: 1840

Ownership: James & John Mill

39. Rosebank[29]

Pronunciation: ROSE-bank

Founded: 1817

Closed: 1993

Ownership: Scottish Malt Distillers Ltd., a subsidiary of Distillers Company Ltd., which became part of United Distillers and Vintners, a subsidiary of Diageo Plc

Water Source: Carrow Valley Reservoir

40. Seggie

Founded: 1810

Closed: 1860

Ownership: John Haig & Co.

41. St. Magdalene[30]

Founded: 1753

Closed: 1983

Ownership: Scottish Malt Distillers, a subsidiary of Distillers Company Ltd., which became part of United Distillers and Vintners, a subsidiary of Diageo Plc

Water Source: Loch Lomond

42. Strathmore[31]

Founded: 1957

Closed: 1980

Ownership: Distillers Company Ltd., which became part of United Distillers and Vintners, a subsidiary of Diageo Plc

43 Sunbury

Founded: 1813

Closed: 1856

Ownership: James Stein & Co.

---

[29]Definitely a single malt whisky distillery. Master of Malt (http://www.masterofmalt.com/distilleries/rosebank-whisky-distillery/) has a listing of different Rosebank Single Malt Scotch Whisky bottlings by Diageo and independent bottlers.

[30]Definitely a single malt whisky distillery. Master of Malt (http://www.masterofmalt.com/distilleries/st-magdalene-whisky-distillery/) has listings for official and independent bottlings of St. Magdalene Single Malt Scotch Whisky under the St. Magdalene and the Linlithgow brand names.

[31]Definitely a single malt whisky distillery—at least before 1960, when the distillery started producing grain instead of single malt whisky. Source: http://www.buxrud.se/samling.htm.

44. Tambowie[32]

Founded: 1825

Closed: 1914

Ownership: Tambowie Distillery Co.

Water Source: Tambowie Hills

45. Yardheads

Founded: 1825

Closed: 1884

Ownership: Alexander Law (built it, but he was not the last owner)

SPEYSIDE

There are 10 closed Speyside malt distilleries on record.

1. Auchorachan

Founded: before 1790

Closed: 1852

Ownership: William Gordon

2. Coleburn[33]

Founded: 1896

Closed: 1985

Ownership: Distillers Company Ltd., which became part of United Distillers and Vintners, a subsidiary of Diageo Plc

3. Convalmore[34]

Pronunciation: CON-val-more

Founded: 1894

Deactivated: 1985

Ownership: William Grant & Sons Ltd. owns the physical fa-

---

[32]Most likely a single malt whisky distillery. Whisky Story in its article on Tambowie (retrieved on February 9, 2013, from http://whiskystory.blogspot.com/2010/08/tambowie-distillery.html) mentions in passing a Tambowie "pure malt" bottling by the Vintage Malt Whisky Company.

[33]Definitely a single malt whisky distillery. Master of Malt (http://www.masterofmalt.com/distilleries/coleburn-whisky-distillery/, accessed on February 10, 2013) has listings for a Diageo and independent bottlings of Coleburn Single Malt Scotch Whisky.

[34]Definitely a single malt whisky distillery. Master of Malt (http://www.masterofmalt.com/distilleries/convalmore-whisky-distillery/, accessed on February 10, 2013) has listings for independent bottlings and an official expression of Convalmore Single Malt Scotch Whisky.

cilities; Scottish Malt Distillers (a subsidiary of Distillers Company Ltd., which became part of United Distillers and Vintners, a subsidiary of Diageo Plc) owns the Convalmore brand

4. Dallas Dhu[35]

Pronunciation: Dallas Doo

Founded: 1899

Closed: 1983

Ownership: Distillers Company Ltd., which became part of United Distillers and Vintners, a subsidiary of Diageo Plc

Water Source: Altyre Burn (known locally as the Scourie Burn)

5. Delnabo

Founded: 1830s

Closed: 1858

Ownership: George Smith

Note: This distillery was also known as Cairngorm, and it was renamed that by the Smiths when they took over in 1850. It's also supposedly the same as the Smiths' other distillery, Glenavon.

6. Glen Cawdor / Glencawdor

Founded: 1898

Closed: 1927

Ownership: John Haig & Co. Ltd.

Water Source: Local springs

7. Parkmore

Founded: 1894

Closed: 1988

Ownership: Highland Distillers Plc, which has been acquired by The Edrington Group

8. Pittyvaich

Pronunciation: PITTY-vake

Founded: 1975

Closed: 1993

Ownership: (since 1987) United Distillers and Vintners, a subsidiary of Diageo Plc

---

[35]Definitely a single malt whisky distillery. Master of Malt (http://www.masterofmalt.com/distilleries/dallas-dhu-whisky-distillery/, accessed on February 10, 2013) has listings for independent bottlings of Dallas Dhu Single Malt Scotch Whisky.

Water Source: Balliemore & Convalleys springs

9. Tochineal

Founded: 1825

Closed: 1871

Ownership: Alexander Wilson & Co.

10. Towiemore

Founded: 1896

Closed: 1930

Ownership: Scottish Malt Distillers, a subsidiary of Distillers Company Ltd., which became part of United Distillers and Vintners, a subsidiary of Diageo Plc

ISLAY

There are 14 closed malt distilleries on record in the protected whisky locality of Islay.

1. Ardenistiel

Founded: 1837

Closed: 1866 (when William Hunter went bankrupt and the distillery was sold to Laphroaig)

Ownership: William Hunter (when it closed); Laphroaig now owns the site and uses it for its offices and warehouses.

2. Ardmore / Lagavulin 2

Founded: 1817

Closed: 1835

Ownership: John Johnston

Note: In 1837, this distillery was absorbed into the modern-day Lagavulin distillery.

3. Bridgend

Founded: Unknown

Closed: 1822

Ownership: D. McEachran Junior & Co.

Note: This was supposedly established as Killarow distillery, but was later renamed to Bridgend. However, other accounts indicate that Killarow and Bridgend were two separate distilleries, and that, in 1922, Killarow acquired Bridgend when Bridgend's owner went bankrupt.

4. Daill

Founded: 1814
Closed: 1830s
Ownership: Donald McEachran

5. Glenavullen

Founded: Unknown
Closed: Unknown
Ownership: Unknown

6. Lochindaal / Port Charlotte / Rhinns

Founded: 1829
Closed: 1929
Ownership: Benmore Distilleries Ltd. that was later absorbed by Distillers Company Ltd., which became part of United Distillers and Vintners, a subsidiary of Diageo Plc
Water Source: Lochs of Garroch and Octomore

Note: Bruichladdich Distillery Co. Ltd., which is now owned by Pernod Ricard, has acquired the site of the Lochindaal distillery. It plans to and has already suc-cessfully obtained planning permission to reopen the Lochindaal distillery—this time as the Port Charlotte distillery.[36] Said reopening is slated for 2016. Inverleven distillery's distilling equipment has already been transported to Islay.

7. Lossit

Founded: 1821
Closed: 1860
Ownership: John C. Stewart

8. Malt Mill

Founded: 1908
Closed: 1960
Ownership: Mackie & Co. (Distillers) Ltd.

Note: This distillery was absorbed by the Lagavulin distillery in 1962.

9. Mulindry / Mulendry

Founded: 1826
Closed: 1831
Ownership: John Sinclair

---

[36]This is according to Islay Info (http://www.islayinfo.com/islay_port_charlotte_distillery.html and http://blog.islayinfo.com/article.php/islay_lochindaal_distillery, accessed on February 10, 2013).

10. Newton

Founded: 1818
Closed: 1837
Ownership: Thomas Pattison

11. Octomore

Founded: 1816
Closed: 1852
Ownership: Thomas Pattison

12. Port Ellen[37]

Pronunciation: port-ELlen
Founded: 1825
Closed: 1983
Ownership: Scottish Malt Distillers (which formed part of Distillers Company Ltd., later becoming part of United Distillers and Vintners, a subsidiary of Diageo Plc)
Water Source: Leorin Lochs

13. Tallant

Founded: 1821

Closed: 1852
Ownership: John Johnston

14. Upper Cragabus

Founded: Unknown
Closed: Unknown
Ownership: Unknown

CAMPBELTOWN

There are 33 closed Campbeltown malt distilleries on record.

1. Albyn

Founded: 1830
Closed: 1927
Ownership: W. McKersie & Co.
Water Source: Crosshill Loch

2. Ardlussa

Founded: 1879
Closed: 1923 (liquidated 1927)
Ownership: West Highland Malt Distilleries Ltd.
Water Source: Guillielands Burn

---

[37]Definitely a single malt whisky distillery. Master of Malt (http://www.masterofmalt.com/distilleries/port-ellen-whisky-distillery/, accessed on February 10, 2013) has listings for official releases and independent bottlings of Port Ellen Single Malt Scotch Whisky.

3. Argyll / McKinnon's Distillery (on Lorne St.)

Founded: 1827

Closed: 1844

Ownership: Duncan McKinnon & Co.

4. Argyll (on Longrow)[38]

Founded: 1844

Closed: 1923

Ownership: Distillers Company Ltd., which became part of United Distillers and Vintners, a subsidiary of Diageo Plc

Water Source: A source on site

5. Ballegreggan

Founded: Unknown

Closed: Unknown

Ownership: William Campbell

6. Benmore

Founded: 1868

Closed: 1927

Ownership: Distillers Company Ltd., which became part of United Distillers and Vintners, a subsidiary of Diageo Plc

Water Source: Wells on site

Note: According to a listing at Master of Malt (accessed on February 10, 2013, from http://www.masterofmalt.com/whiskies/benmore/benmore-special-reserve-blended-scotch whisky-1970s-whisky/), it appears that the name Benmore is now used as a brand name for a blended Scotch whisky.

7. Broombrae

Founded: 1833

Closed: 1834

Ownership: Edward Robertson

8. Burnside

Founded: 1825

Closed: 1924

Ownership: Burnside Distillery Co.

---

[38]Beinn Bhuide Holdings appears to have a bottling of Argyll Single Malt Scotch Whisky. A 12-year-old Argyll single malt was sold for £40 at http://www.scotchwhiskyauctions.com/store/product/48_the-20th-auction-runs-until-sunday-december-02-2012/8441_020117-argyll-single-malt-12-year-old/ (accessed February 10, 2013).

9. Caledonian

Founded: 1823
Closed: 1851
Ownership: James Johnstone

10. Campbeltown

Founded: 1815
Closed: 1924
Ownership: Campbeltown Distillery Co.
Water Source: Water main from Crosshill Loch

11. Dalaruan

Founded: 1824
Closed: 1922
Ownership: Charles Colvill, David Colville, Daniel Greenlees, John McMurchy

12. Dalintober

Founded: 1832
Closed: 1925
Ownership: West Highland Malt Distilleries Ltd.

13. Drumore

Founded: 1834
Closed: 1847

Ownership: Templeton, Fulton & Co.

14. Glen Nevis

Founded: 1877
Closed: 1923
Ownership: West Highland Malt Distilleries Ltd.
Water Source: Crosshill Loch

15. Glengyle

Founded: 1873
Closed: 1925
Ownership: West Highland Malt Distilleries Ltd.

Note: This was the original Glengyle distillery in Campbeltown. It is succeeded on the same site by Mitchell's Glengyle Distillery, which was opened in 2004 and bottles and sells Single Malt Scotch Whisky under the Kilkerran brand name.

16. Glenramskill

Founded: unknown (supposedly founded before 1828)
Closed: 1852
Ownership: Robert Ralston

17. Glenside

Founded: 1830
Closed: 1926
Ownership: Train & McIntyre
Water Source: Aucha Lochy

18. Hazelburn

Founded: 1796
Closed: 1925
Ownership: White Horse Distillers Ltd. (this was later absorbed by Distillers Company Ltd., which became part of United Distillers and Vintners, a subsidiary of Diageo Plc)

Note: The Hazelburn distillery, even though it is closed, is not forgotten because "Hazelburn" is one of the brands of single malt whisky produced by the Springbank Distillery.

19. Highland

Founded: 1827
Closed: 1852
Ownership: Dawson & Baird

20. Kinloch

Founded: 1823
Closed: 1926

Ownership: Duncan MacCallum
Water Source: Sources on site

21. Kintyre

Founded: 1825
Closed: 1920
Ownership: John Ross & Co.

22. Lochhead / Lochead

Founded: 1824
Closed: 1928
Ownership: Benmore Distilleries Ltd. (this was later absorbed by Distillers Company Ltd., which became part of United Distillers and Vintners, a subsidiary of Diageo Plc)

23. Lochruan

Founded: 1835
Closed: 1925
Ownership: Distillers Company Ltd., which became part of United Distillers and Vintners, a subsidiary of Diageo Plc
Water Source: Lochruan

24. Lochside

Founded: 1830
Closed: 1852
Ownership: Gilkinson & Hunter

25. Longrow

Founded: 1824
Closed: 1896
Ownership: William & James Greenlees

Note: Even though this distillery is closed, its name lives on. Longrow is Springbank's name for its double-distilled, heavily peated single malt whisky.

26. Meadowburn

Founded: 1824
Closed: 1886
Ownership: Robert Colvill & Co.

27. Mossfield

Founded: 1834
Closed: 1837
Ownership: Harvey & Hunter

28. Mountain Dew

Founded: 1834
Closed: 1837
Ownership: Peter Watson & Co.

29. Rieclachan

Founded: 1825
Closed: 1934
Ownership: Wylie, Mitchell & Co.
Water Source: Crosshill Loch

30. Springside

Founded: 1830
Closed: 1926
Ownership: John Colvill & Co.
Water Source: Crosshill Loch

31. Toberanrigh

Founded: 1834
Closed: 1860
Ownership: John Mitchell

32. Union

Founded: 1826
Closed: 1850
Ownership: John Grant & Co.

33. West Highland

Founded: 1830

Closed: 1860

Ownership: Archibald Andrew and Andrew Montgomery

LIST OF DEACTIVATED DISTILLERIES

Mothballing refers to the business practice of ceasing continuous production but keeping equipment and other production facilities in working order, so that such equipment and facilities can be used when needed (i.e., for on-demand or occasional production). Thus, deactivated distilleries—while they are not actively producing whisky at the moment—are capable of resuming production anytime their owners decide to do so.

Below is a list of the three deactivated Single Malt Scotch Whisky distilleries on record:

1. Caperdonich

Pronunciation: CA-per-DO-nik

Founded: 1898

Ownership: Chivas Brothers, a subsidiary of Pernod Ricard

Region: Speyside

Water Source: Caperdonich Burn

2. Glen Keith

Founded: 1958

Ownership: Chivas Brothers, a subsidiary of Pernod Ricard

Region: Speyside

Water Source: Source on Balloch Hill

3. Imperial

Founded: 1897

Ownership: Allied Domecq, owned by Pernod Ricard

Region: Speyside

Water Source: Ballintomb Burn

Endnotes

i   Whiskies of Scotland. (n.d.). Ailsa Bay. Date accessed: February 10, 2013 (http://www.whiskiesofscotland.com/distillery/ailsa-bay).

ii   Ayrshire Rivers Trust. (n.d.). River Girvan. Date accessed: February 10, 2013 (http://www.ayrshireriverstrust.org/river-girvan.htm).

iii   University of Edinburgh. (n.d.). Annandale. Date accessed: February 10, 2013 (http://www.dcs.ed.ac.uk/home/jhb/whisky/smws/138.html).

iv   Annandale Distillery. (n.d.). 4th Whisky Era – Annandale Distillery Company (2007). Date accessed: February 10, 2013 (http://www.annandaledistillery.co.uk/whisky/past/4th-whisky-era/).

v   Ulf Buxrud. (2000). Lost Scotch Malt Whisky Distilleries 1885-1945. Date accessed: February 2, 2013 (http://www.buxrud.se/lost.htm).

vi   Daftmill Distillery. (n.d.). About Daftmill. Date accessed: February 10, 2013 (http://www.daftmill.com/index.php/about-daftmill).

vii   Gavin D. Smith. (n.d.). Daftmill Distillery, *Whisky Pages*. Date accessed: February 10, 2013 (http://www.whisky-pages.com/stories/daftmill.htm). It must be noted that this figure is what the distillery is technically capable of producing and may or may not match actual production.

MOST UTILIZED REFERENCES ON CLOSED DISTILLERIES

Johannes van den Heuvel. (n.d.). Malt Madness. (http://www.maltmadness.com).

The Lost Distilleries of Scotland. (n.d.). The Lost Distilleries of Scotland. (http://lostdistillery.com).

Ulf Buxrud. (2000). Lost Scotch Malt Whisky Distilleries 1885-1945. (http://www.buxrud.se/lost.htm).

University of Edinburgh. (n.d.). The Edinburgh Malt Whisky Tour. (http://www.dcs.ed.ac.uk/home/jhb/whisky/index.html).

Worm Tub (n.d.). Distilleries. (http://www.wormtub.com/distilleries.php).

OTHER REFERENCES FOR CLOSED DISTILLERIES

Alex Kraaijeveld. (2004). Did Rabbie have a favourite dram? The World Burns Club. Date accessed: February 2, 2013 (http://www.cobbler.plus.com/wbc/expert/did_rabbie_have_a%20_favourite_dram.htm).

Associated Newspapers Ltd. (October 19, 2006). Is this the world's oldest bottle of whisky? Mail Online, The Daily Mail. Date accessed: February 10, 2013 (http://www.dailymail.co.uk/news/article-411415/Is-worlds-oldest-bottle-whisky.html) (used as reference for Delnabo).

Brian Townsend. (1997). Scotch Missed: The Lost Distilleries of Scotland, extract reproduced in "A Brief History of the Grange Distillery" on Burntisland.net. Date accessed: February 10, 2013 (http://www.burntisland.net/distillery.htm).

David Landau. (July 7, 2009). BL O/188/09. Date accessed: February 1, 2013 (http://www.ipo.gov.uk/types/tm/t-os/t-find/t-challenge-decision-results/o18809.pdf).

Evanton Oral History Project. (January 28, 2010). Evanton Village – with sections on Glenskiach Distillery, Mackenzie's Garage, Mills, Transport. Date accessed: February 1, 2013 (http://www.spanglefish.com/evantonoralhistoryproject/documents/EVANTON%20VILLAGE%20BOOKLET%203(2).doc. p.23-26).

F. Paul Pacult. (2011). A Doble Scotch: How Chivas Regal and The Glenlivet Became Global Icons. John Wiley Sons. Date accessed: February 3, 2013 (http://books-google.com.ph/books?id=8fDXM4IIGsC&pg-=PT88&lpg=T88&dq=james-+mchardy+126&source=-bl&ots=yecBOtN0W&sig=enLhidYH7Z1fNeSMI00FHTITUU&hl=en&sa=&ei=FIkNUYz4NMuXiQeA1o4BA&redir_esc=y#v=onepage&q=james%2mchardy&f=false).

Ian R. Mitchell. (n.d.). The one that got away, Whisky Magazine. Date accessed: February 3, 2013 (http://www.whiskymag.com/magazine/issue65/12008000.html).

John Porter. (April 1975). In Search of the Real Old Mountain Dew, Caithness Field Club Bulletin (as reprinted at Caithness.org "The Real Mountain Dew"). Date accessed: February 1, 2013 (http://www.caithness.org/history/articles/therealmountaindew.htm).

John Porter. (1977). Whisky & Halkirk: Ben Morven Distillery, early 20th century, Halkirk and its Highland Games. Halkirk Athletic Club. (Reprinted at ThisIsHalkirk.co.uk "About Halkirk – Whisky Distillery"). Date accessed: February 1, 2013 (http://www.hisishalkirk.co.uk/about/whisky.htm).

Kennetpans Distillery. (n.d.). A Brief History of Kennetpans, The History of Kennetpans. Date accessed: February 10, 2013 (http://www.kennetpans.info/index.php?option=com_content&vrticle&id=133&Itemid=232).

Kennetpans Distillery. (n.d.). Ardenistiel Distillery, The History of Kennetpans. Date accessed: February 10, 2013 (http://www.kennetpans.info/index.php?option=com_content&view=article&id=364:ardenistiel-distillery&catid=55:stein-distilleries&Itemid=548).

Scotch Malt Whisky. (n.d.). Millburn Single Malt Scotch Whisky. Date accessed: February 1, 2013 (http://www.scotchmaltwhisky.co.uk/millburn.htm).

Scotland: Whisky and Distilleries. (n.d.). History of Scotch Whisky before 1787. Date accessed: February 8, 2013 (http://www.whisky-distilleries.info/HistoireAvant1787_EN.shtml).

Scotlands Places. (n.d.). Kennetpans Distillery. Date accessed: February 10, 2013 (http://www.scotlandsplaces.gov.uk/search_item/index.php?service=-RCAHMS&id=48117).

The Scotch Whisky Experience. (n.d.). The origin of Scotch. Date accessed: February 2, 2013 (http://www.scotchwhiskyexperience.co.uk/scotch-whisky/whisky-history.php).

The Whisky Exchange. (n.d.). Killyloch (Moffat). Date accessed: February 9, 2013 (http://www.thewhiskyexchange.com/B-40-Killyloch_(Moffat).aspx#more).

The Whisky Portal. (n.d.). Bank Distillery. Date accessed: February 10, 2013 (http://www.whiskyportal.com/distillery.asp?DistilleryID=430&DistilleryName=Bank+Distillery).

The Whisky Portal. (n.d.). Geise Distillery. Date accessed: January 30, 2013 (http://www.whiskyportal.com/distillery.asp?DistilleryID=450&DistilleryName=Geise+Distillery).

The Whisky Portal. (n.d.). Milltown Distillery. Date accessed: February 1, 2013 (http://www.whiskyportal.com/distillery.asp?DistilleryID=718&DistilleryName=Milltown+Distillery).

Tom Keller. (July 2009). The Sound of Whisky (2) – Robert Burns: Freedom an' Whisky Gang Thegither, Folk World. Issue 39 07/2009. Date accessed: February 2, 2013 (http://www.folkworld.de/39/e/burns1.html).

Whisky Story. (August 13, 2010). Tambowie Distillery. Date accessed: February 9, 2013 (http://whisky-story.blogspot.com/2010/08/tambowie-distillery.html.)

Whisky Story. (September 8, 2010). Glenifer Distillery, near Paisley. Date accessed: February 10,

2013 (http://lostdistillery.com/02lowlands-north-west/glen-patrick.html#more).

Whisky Story. (October 21, 2010). Glenside Distillery, Campbeltown. Date accessed: February 10, 2013 (http://whiskystory.blogspot.com/2010/10/glenside-distillery-campbeltown.html).

Whisky Story. (November 4, 2010). Campbeltown Distillery. Date accessed: February 10, 2013 (http://whiskystory.blogspot.com/2010/11/campbeltown-distillery.html).

Whisky Story. (November 7, 2010). Argyll Distillery, Campbeltown. Date accessed: February 10, 2013 (http://whiskystory.blogspot.com/2010/11/argyll-distillery-campbeltown.html).

Whisky Story. (December 18, 2010). Port Ellen Distillery, Islay. Date accessed: February 10, 2013 (http://whiskystory.blogspot.com/2010/12/port-ellen-distillery-islay.html).

Whisky Story. (February 12, 2011). Glendarroch Distillery, Ardrishaig. Date accessed: February 9, 2013 (http://whiskystory blogspot.com/2011/02/glendarroch-distillery-ardrishaig.html).

Whisky Story. (March 30, 2011). Gerston Distillery, Halkirk. Date accessed: February 1, 2013 (http://whiskystory.blogspot.com/2011/03/gerston-distillery-halkirk.html).

Whisky.com. (n.d.). Glen Albyn Single Malt Scotch Whisky. Date accessed: February 1, 2013 (http://www.whisky.com/brands/glen_albyn_brand.html).

Whisky.com. (n.d.). Littlemill Single Malt Scotch Whisky. Date accessed: February 9, 2013 (http://www.whisky.com/brands/littlemill_brand.html).

Whisky-News.com. (n.d.). The Glenlivet. Date accessed: February 10, 2013 (http://www.whisky-news.com/En/distilleries/Glenlivet.html (used as reference for Delnabo).

Chapter VIII

Scotch Whisky Glossary

What are maltster, middle cut, washback, and angel's share? Start talking like a Scotch Whisky connoisseur by learning the language of Single Malt Scotch.

ABV
Acronym for Alcohol by Volume.

Age
Refers to the number of years a Scotch Whisky has spent maturing or aging in an oak cask.

Age Statement
Found on the Scotch Whisky bottle, this is the distiller's declaration of a Scotch Whisky's age.

A Scotch Whisky's age statement is the same as its actual age if the Scotch Whisky is a Single Cask Edition.

If the Scotch Whisky in the bottle is a blend of two or more whiskies from different casks that were filled in different years, such Scotch Whisky's age statement is equivalent to the age of the youngest whisky used in the blend.

To illustrate, if a distillery combines its 12-year-old Malt Scotch Whisky with its 13-year-old Malt Scotch Whisky for a bottling, the resulting product is a 12-year-old Single Malt Scotch Whisky. The age statement on the bottle of such whisky, therefore, will be something like "Twelve Years Old" or "Aged 12 Years."

Aging

Refers to the maturation stage in Scotch Whisky production. At this stage, the final distillate (or the liquid spirit produced after spirit still distillation) is placed in an oak cask. There it is allowed to mature for a period of no less than three years. Only after aging can Scotch Whisky be bottled.

Alcohol by Volume

The measure of a Scotch Whisky's alcoholic strength. This is the percentage of pure alcohol present in a Scotch Whisky. The higher a Scotch's Whisky's Alcohol by Volume, the more alcoholic it is. Scotch Whisky must have an alcoholic strength of at least 40% (i.e., 40% ABV).

As per the Scotch Whisky Regulations of 2009, a Scotch Whisky's Alcohol by Volume is determined at a temperature of 20 degrees Celsius and is calculated by dividing the volume of pure alcohol by the whisky's total volume, and then multiplying the quotient by 100, there-fore expressing the ABV as a percentage.

Alembic Still

See Pot Still.

Angel's Share

Whisky that evaporates from the cask during the maturation period. Oak casks are not airtight containers, so while whisky is maturing, it evaporates at an average rate of 1-2% per year. Most of the volume lost during maturation is water, especially when whisky is matured in dry cellars. The angel's share, however, can also contain alcohol; thus, maturation can lead to a slight but gradual reduction in a Scotch Whisky's alcoholic strength.

Aroma

The scent of a Scotch Whisky. A whisky's aromas are attributable to its chemical makeup. As per the Scotch Whisky Regulations of 2009, an authentic Scotch Whisky's aromas must be determined by the raw materials and the method of production used.

Barley

Barley—scientific name *Hordeum vulgare*—is a cereal grain. Malted barley is one of the essential ingredients of Scotch whisky.

Barrel

A barrel, in the context of Scotch Whisky production, is a cask with a capacity of more or less 175 liters. A Scotch Whisky barrel is always made of oak.

Batch Distillation

The process of distilling Scotch Whisky by batches. In batch distillation, a fixed amount of raw materials (e.g., low wines in the case of spirit still distillation) is fed into the still and distilled completely (or as completely as possible). The distillate is then removed before another batch of raw materials is fed into the still. In batch distillation, the raw materials are limited so the amount of materials in the pot decreases, and the nature of these materials' composition changes as the distillation progresses.

Bottling Year

The year the Scotch Whisky is bottled. A whisky's bottling year is different from its age. Aging can take place only in oak casks, so the years a Scotch Whisky spends in the bottle no longer count toward its age. Thus, a 12-year-old Scotch bottled in 2008 remains a 12-year-old Scotch, even if it is opened and consumed in 2010.

Blend

This is a general term used to refer to any whisky that is a blend of two or more whiskies, whatever their types, ages, methods/equipment of production, and distilleries/production regions of origin. This should not be confused with Blended Scotch Whisky, Blended Grain Scotch Whisky, and Blended Malt Scotch Whisky. Although these are actually blends, they are still official categories of Scotch Whisky and thus have much narrower definitions.

Blended Grain Scotch Whisky

Made by blending two or more Single Grain Scotch Whiskies from two or more distilleries in Scotland. This is also known simply as Blended Grain Scotch.

Blended Malt Scotch Whisky

Made by blending two or more Single Malt Scotch Whiskies from two or more distilleries in Scotland. This is also known simply as Blended Malt Scotch.

Blended Malt Whisky

In the context of Scotch Whisky, this is synonymous to Blended Malt Scotch Whisky. The term blended malt whisky is traditionally synonymous to "vatted malt whisky" and "pure malt whisky." Whiskies simply labeled as "malt whisky," moreover, are most likely to be blended malt whiskies.

Blended Scotch Whisky

Made by blending one or more Single Malt Scotch Whiskies AND one or more Single Grain Scotch Whiskies. This blend of single grain and single malt whiskies is also known simply as Blended Scotch.

Blended Whisky

See Blend.

Blending

Combining two or more whiskies to come up with a blend or blended whisky.

Brewer Maltster

A brewery that makes malt for its own brewing needs (i.e., to produce beer).

Butt

A type of cask with a 500-liter capacity (more or less), which is approximately twice the capacity of a hogshead—another type of cask. A butt is the cask type used by Sherry producers, and used Sherry butts are a popular cask choice among Scotch Whisky producers.

Campbeltown

One of the protected whisky localities in Scotland.

Caramel Coloring

See Plain Caramel Coloring.

Cask

The container used for aging Scotch Whisky. It is made of oak, is almost always second-hand, and has a capacity of 700 liters or less.

Different types of oak casks are used by Scotch Whisky producers. These include oak barrels (with a capacity of plus or minus 175 liters), oak butts (with a capacity of plus or minus 500 liters), and oak hogsheads (with a capacity of plus or minus 250 liters).

Generally, the second-hand oak casks distilleries use in Scotch Whisky aging used to contain other alcoholic beverages such as:

- Sherry (fortified wine from Jerez, Spain)
- Port (fortified wine from the Douro Valley of Portugal)
- Madeira (fortified wine from the Madeira Islands, Portugal)
- Bordeaux (wine from the Bordeaux wine region)
- Cognac (grape brandy from the Cognac appellation in France)
- Calvados (apple brandy from the Calvados appellation in France)
- Bourbon (corn whiskey from the USA)
- Beer

The most popular oak casks in Scotland are Sherry butts (butts that used to hold Sherry) and Bourbon barrels (barrels that used to hold Bourbon).

Cask Strength

Cask strength refers to the alcoholic strength of Scotch Whisky in-cask.

Cask Strength Scotch Whisky

Scotch Whisky that has been bottled direct from the cask, so its ABV is at cask strength. In other words, cask strength Scotch Whisky is whisky that has not been diluted prior to bottling.

Cereal

Cereal or cereal grains are a type of grass or weed cultivated for their fruit seeds. Barley, wheat, millet, rye, sorghum, rice, and oats are examples of cereal grains.

Charring

Oak casks undergo a charring or toasting process, especially if they are to be used for storing/aging Bourbon, the American corn whiskey. The cooper (the oak cask assembler) puts the partially constructed oak cask over a small wood fire. This chars or toasts the wood on the inside portion of the cask. Charring levels vary depending on the requirements of the wine maker or the spirit distiller. An oak cask may have light, medium or heavy char.

Chill Filtering
See Chill Filtration.

Chill Filtration
Chill filtration is a cosmetic process, done by some Scotch Whisky producers to ensure that their whisky will not become clouded or hazy when chilled or diluted with ice water before consumption. Haziness or cloudiness upon dilution or chilling usually occurs when a Scotch Whisky is below 46% ABV. Thus, Scotch Whisky producers usually do not chill-filter whiskies that are at 46% or greater ABV.

In chill filtration, Scotch Whisky is first chilled to a temperature of -10 to 4 degrees Celsius. The low temperature causes the oily or fatty compounds in the whisky to precipitate or clump together. The chilled whisky is then passed through a fine filter so that the precipitates or the oily/fatty residues can be filtered out.

Coastal Scotch Whisky
Scotch Whisky that has been aged in a warehouse near the sea. The term Coastal Scotch Whisky is also used to refer to Scotch Whisky produced by distilleries located along the coast. It is believed that Coastal Scotch Whiskies manifest distinct saline or other "sea" flavors (e.g., seaweed flavor), which are deemed to be the influence of the nearby seawater.

Coastal Whisky
See Coastal Scotch Whisky.

Coffey Still
See Column Still.

Column Still
A type of still used in the continuous distillation of whisky. A column still continuously produces distillate from a continuously replenished feedstock, employing the fractional distillation method to produce distillate with exceptionally high alcohol content. The column still is also known as the Coffey still, patent still, continuous still, or columnar still.

A column still provides a cost-efficient way of distilling whisky. Thus, Scotch Whisky made using a column still is typically more affordable than whisky made using a pot still. Note, however, that while the column still may be used in distilling Single Grain Scotch Whisky, it may not be used in the distillation of Single Malt Scotch Whisky. Single Malt Scotch Whisky must be distilled only in batches and using pot stills.

Columnar Still
See Column Still.

Condensation
That stage in the distillation process when alcoholic vapors are converted to liquid spirit (i.e., the distillate).

Condenser
That part of the still that lowers the temperature of the alcoholic vapors so they will condense into liquid spirit.

Congeners
Chemical compounds that are byproducts of the fermentation process. Congeners are supposedly responsible for the taste, aroma, and color of alcoholic beverages such as Scotch Whisky.

Continuous Distillation
See Fractional Distillation.

Continuous Still
See Column Still.

Cooper
The assembler or maker of oak casks.

Corn
The main ingredient used in the production of Bourbon whiskey. It may be added to malted barley in the production of Single Grain Scotch Whisky.

Cut
A fraction of the liquid spirit produced during spirit still distillation. The liquid spirit leaving the spirit still has three cuts: the first cut (i.e., foreshots), the middle cut (i.e., new make or heart of the run), and the third cut (i.e., feints).

Distillate

The liquid product of distillation. In wash still distillation, low wines are the distillate. In spirit still distillation, the distillate is liquid spirit (which can be classified into three cuts, one of which is ready for casking).

Distillation

The process of breaking a mixture down to its individual components according to the differences in these components' volatility (i.e., tendency to vaporize). Scotch Whisky is an alcoholic beverage produced through batch or continuous distillation.

Distiller Maltster

A distillery that makes malt for its own distilling needs (i.e., to produce Malt Scotch Whisky).

Distillery

A distillery is an establishment or a facility that produces distilled spirits such as Scotch Whisky.

Draff

The deposits or residues produced after the mash has undergone constant and prolonged stirring in the mash tun. These are the solid particulates left in the mash tun after the wort has been removed. Accumulated draff is dried then sold as animal food.

Dram

The traditional measure of volume for Scotch Whisky. One dram of Scotch Whisky is not the same as the regulation fluid dram (which is equivalent to approximately 3.7 ml or 1/8 fluid ounces). In fact, a "wee dram" of Scotch Whisky is, not by any measure, a small amount; it can actually be 10 times as much as one regulation fluid dram. A dram of Scotch Whisky can be equal to 36.97 ml of whisky.

Drum Malting

A specific method of producing malted grain. In drum barley malting, moist barley is placed in a drum that rotates gently but continuously until the barley germinates and becomes malted barley.

Endogenous Enzyme Systems

Enzyme systems developed or grown from within. In the context of Scotch Whisky production, only endogenous enzyme systems may be used to prepare the sugar-rich substance that will be fermented then later distilled. In other words, a Scotch Whisky producer cannot add artificial enzymes to their grains to convert their grains' starch content to sugar. The enzymes that may act on the grains must be developed from within—that is, developed by the grains themselves.

To create such "endogenous enzyme systems," Scotch Whisky producers malt their grains. The grains are first soaked in water then allowed to germinate. As the grains sprout, they naturally develop enzymes that convert their starch content to sugar, which they need to support their growth.

Excise Warehouse

An excise warehouse is a warehouse used for storing products that are subject to excise duty or tax. Scotch Whisky is subject to excise taxes; thus, the Scotch Whisky Regulations of 2009 requires that Scotch Whiskies be aged in an excise warehouse or in any other place approved by Her Majesty's Revenue & Customs department.

Feedstock

The raw materials fed to or distilled through a still.

Feint Receiver

That part of the spirit still to which the feints are directed and in which they are held until they can be mixed with the next batch of low wines.

Feints

The third or final cut or part of the spirit run produced by spirit still distillation. This is the liquid spirit's weakest fraction. It is collected in the feint receiver and later mixed with the next batch of low wines to be distilled in the spirit still.

Fermentation

Conversion of sugar to alcohol through yeast action. In Scotch Whisky production, fermentation is initiated through the addition of yeast to the wort in the washback. The yeast consumes the sugars in the wort, producing alcohol as a byproduct. After approximately two to five days, fermentation is completed. The wash, a mildly alcoholic liquid, is the end-product of fermenting the wort.

Floor Malting

A type of malting method used in some Scotch Whisky distilleries. In floor malting, the germinating barley grains (i.e., barley that has already begun to sprout) are spread out on the floor and left there for a period of one to two weeks. To aerate the grains and ensure even development, the grains are regularly turned with a paddle throughout the entire malting period.

Foreshots

The first cut or the first fraction of the spirit run produced during spirit still distillation. This first cut is considered unusable (i.e., not ready for casking) since it has a very high alcoholic strength and contains impurities. The foreshots are collected in a receiver, and then combined with the next batch of low wines to be distilled in the spirit still.

Fractional Distillation

The type of distillation method used in making Grain Scotch Whisky. In fractional distillation, the still produces a continuous stream of distillate as it is continuously fed or charged with feedstock. A column still is used in fractional distillation.

Gauger

An exciseman or a revenue officer in charge of inspecting goods subject to excise tax. Scotch Whisky is a commodity subject to excise tax, so it must undergo a gauger's inspection.

Germination

The stage during which a plant grows or sprouts from a seed. Germination is essential to the malting process. Through germination, cereal grains produce endogenous enzyme systems that convert the grains' starch content to sugar. In other words, germination makes the conversion of starch-rich cereal grains into sugar-rich malt possible.

Grain

See Cereal.

Grain Distillery

In Scotland, a grain distillery is a distillery that produces Grain Scotch Whisky.

Grain Scotch Whisky

Scotch Whisky that has been made using a combination of whole grains (malted barley plus supplementary grains, which can be malted or unmalted) and water. This can be Single Grain Scotch Whisky or Blended Grain Scotch Whisky.

Grain Whisky

See Grain Scotch Whisky.

Grist

Grist is milled, malted barley. It is rich in sugar and has a flour-like consistency.

Guaranteed Age Whisky

Scotch Whisky that has an age statement on the label.

Heart of the Run

See Middle Cut.

Highland

One of the protected/controlled whisky production regions in Scotland.

Hogshead

A type of cask with a capacity of more or less 250 liters. Hogshead casks used in whisky production are always made of oak.

Hydrometer

The instrument used to measure the alcoholic strength of Scotch Whisky. A hydrometer may be installed in the spirit safe to help the stillman gauge the alcoholic strength of the liquid spirit leaving the spirit still.

Islands

A part of the Highland whisky-production region. While this is a significant whisky-production area, it is not recognized as one of the protected/controlled whisky production regions in Scotland. Scotch Whisky distilleries from the Islands must use "Highland," not "Island," if they want to indicate their whisky's geographical origin on their labels.

Islay

An Island in Western Scotland, this is one of the protected whisky localities in Scotland.

Kiln

See Malt Kiln.

Legs

The streaks of whisky that form on the side of the glass after a bit of swirling. A professional whisky taster can use the legs to guess a Scotch Whisky's age or body. According to the Scotch Whisky Association, if a Scotch Whisky's legs are thin, the Scotch Whisky is probably young or light. On the other hand, if a Scotch Whisky's legs are thick or viscous, the Scotch Whisky is probably old or heavy.

Lomond Still

This is Alistair Cunningham's version of the pot still. Like the pot still, it is used in batch distillation—but unlike the pot still, it has a flexible Lyne Arm, the angle of which may be changed to suit the distiller's preferences. The length of the Lomond Still's neck is also flexible. Inside the neck are three plates, the position of which may be changed from vertical to horizontal and vice-versa. Changing the position of the pla-

tes effectively changes the length of the neck and thus the volume of reflux during distillation.

A Scotch Whisky producer, therefore, can make different whisky variants across several runs using just one Lomond Still, even if—for every run—he uses the same ingredients and distills under similar circumstances. All he needs to do is change the length of the neck before distilling a batch of feedstock.

Low Wines

The feedstock used in spirit still distillation. Low wines are produced by running the wash through the wash still.

Lowland

Located in Southern Scotland, this is one of the protected/controlled whisky production regions in Scotland.

Lyne Arm

The pipe (perfectly horizontal or slightly angled) that connects the neck of the still to the still's condenser.

Malt

The sugar-rich end-product of the malting process. In the context of Single Malt Scotch Whisky production, malt refers to malted barley.

Malt Distillery

A distillery that produces malt whisky for its own bottling or for sale to independent bottlers/private collectors as well as makers of blends.

Malt Kiln

The oven used for drying malted grains. After a week (or a couple of weeks) of malting, malted cereal grains are placed in the malt kiln to dry. Drying is necessary to stop the germination process.

Traditionally, malt kilns were heated using a peat fire. The malted grains dried using these traditional malt kilns had a smoky, peaty flavor, which was subsequently passed on to the finished product (the Scotch Whisky). Today, more distilleries use a non-peat-powered malt kiln. However, a distiller with a non-peat malt kiln can give his whisky a distinctly peaty flavor by adding a small amount of peat to his malt kiln's fire. He can also burn peat and blow the peat fire smoke toward the drying malt inside the kiln. In either case, the more peat used, the more peaty the resulting malt (and thus the more peaty the resulting whisky).

Malt Whisky

Whisky made using malted barley grains. Malt Scotch Whisky can be single malt (malt whisky produced by only one distillery) or blended malt (a blend of two or more Single Malt Scotch Whiskies from two or more distilleries).

Malted Barley

Barley that has undergone the malting process. In other words, it has been soaked in water so it can germinate, after which it is placed in a malt kiln to dry. Barley is malted to prepare it for fermentation. Malted barley has higher sugar content than unmalted barley; thus malted barley is more readily fermentable than unmalted barley.

Malted Grain

Cereal grain that has undergone the malting process.

Malting

The process that converts starch-rich grains to sugar-rich grains. There are three basic steps in the malting process. First, the whole grains are steeped or soaked in water. Second, they are laid out on the malting floor or placed inside a malting drum or a Saladin Box, so they can germinate; while there, they are regularly stirred with a paddle (if using a malting floor) or are kept moving through an automated mechanism (if using a malting drum or a Saladin Box) to maximize aeration and ensure the grains' even growth. Third, the grains are dried, using a malt kiln, to stop their germination.

Malting increases the sugar content of cereal grains, because when grains are sprouting or germinating, they convert their starch content to sugar, which they need to fuel plant growth.

Maltster

An entity that makes malt for brewing, distilling, or other purposes. There are three main types of maltsters, according to the Maltsters Association of Great Britain. They are the brewer maltsters, distiller maltsters, and sales maltsters.

Marriage

In the context of Scotch Whisky production, this is the period during which whiskies from different casks are combined in a single vat (i.e., vatted together) so their flavors can harmonize. A marriage requires the use of an oak cask and lasts several months.

Mash

A mixture of grist (milled malted barley) and hot water.

Mash Tun

The metal container where mash is placed and regularly stirred to induce the release of sugars, and thus create the sugar-rich liquid known as the wort.

Mashing

The process of creating mash—that is, adding hot water to the grist.

Master Blender

The specialist responsible for putting together whiskies from different casks. His job is to make or formulate whisky that will be bottled and sold.

Maturation

The stage during which the liquid distillate produced during spirit still distillation is allowed to rest for a period of several years (minimum of three) in an oak cask. Maturation is an important stage in a Scotch Whisky's development. During maturation, Scotch Whisky mellows and develops depth and character. It is also during maturation that Scotch Whisky develops flavors that were not present in the original distillate.

The Scotch Whisky Regulations of 2009 dictates that Scotch Whisky must mature in oak casks with a capacity no greater than 700 liters. It also stipulates that Scotch Whisky maturation must take place in Scotland, in an excise warehouse or any other government-approved place.

Middle Cut

This is the usable part, fraction, or cut of the liquid distillate produced during spirit still distillation. The middle cut has the right alcoholic strength for casking and maturation, so it needs no further distillation. The other cuts (the foreshots and the feints), on the other hand, are collected into separate receivers, so they can be mixed with the next batch of low wines to undergo spirit still distillation.

Moonshine

Illegally produced Scotch Whisky. Moonshine is named such because, traditionally, illegally distilled Scotch Whisky was made at night when smoke from the stills is hard to detect. Moonshine production was particularly rampant when the English Malt Tax was in force.

Mouth-feel

Refers mainly to the texture of whisky inside the mouth.

Neck

Part of the still, this is the column on top of the pot. It is through the neck that alcoholic vapors pass on their way to the Lyne Arm. The height and the diameter of the neck determine which of the alcoholic vapors passing through it will proceed to the Lyne Arm and which will condense prematurely and be returned to the pot as reflux.

New Make

See Middle Cut.

Non-Chill-filtered

Scotch Whisky that has not undergone chill filtration. Normally, 46% or greater ABV Scotch Whiskies are non-chill-filtered.

Nose-Feel

The sensation "felt" by your nose when you sniff a glass of whisky. Different whiskies cause different nose-feels. For instance, an extremely strong whisky (high ABV whisky) may sting or "burn" your nose and leave it feeling numb, while another whisky with lower alcohol content may cause only a mild tingling.

Nosing

The process of evaluating whisky through the nose—that is, sniffing whisky to evaluate its aromas and nose-feel.

Nosing Glass

A special type of glassware used for nosing whisky. Ideally, it should be shaped like a tulip—wide at the bottom and narrow at the rim—so that the whisky inside can be liberally swirled and aerated, but its aromas can be collected and caught at the narrow opening. Ideally, moreover, the whisky snifter should be made of crystal (crystal is very clear, so it is great for visually inspecting whisky), but it should not be cut-crystal, the facets of which can distort a whisky's appearance.

Organic Whisky

Whisky made from organically grown grains or grains grown on "virgin soil" (i.e., soil to which no inorganic fertilizers have been applied) without the aid of inorganic pesticides and insecticides.

Paddle

The device used to turn/stir the germinating grains laid out on the malting floor. The paddle can be manually operated or automated.

Pagoda

The pyramid-shaped roof found on traditional malt ovens or malt kilns. Its design ensures good air intake, thereby improving a malt kiln's performance.

Patent Still

See Column Still.

Peat

The fuel traditionally used to dry malted barley. Some malt producers still use peat when drying malt—but not as the primary heat source.

Plain Caramel Coloring

The name of the specific type of caramel-colored food coloring (color E150a) that Scotch Whisky distillers are permitted to use if they want to enhance the color of their whiskies. As per the provisions of the Scotch Whisky Regulations 2009, only water and/or plain caramel coloring may be added to the final distillate when making Scotch Whisky.

Pot Still

The type of still used for batch distillation, and also the type of still prescribed for producing Single Malt Scotch Whisky. The pot still looks like a sealed, wide-bottomed bowl with a vertically extended, swan-like neck that is connected to a horizontal pipe (the Lyne Arm), which is (in turn) connected to the condenser.

Proof

An alternative measure of alcoholic strength; you may or may not find it on whisky labels. Alcoholic proof or proof spirit used to be the preferred measure of alcoholic strength before the Alcohol by Volume (ABV) measure was developed and widely adopted. In the U.K., ABV is converted to proof spirit using a ratio of 1:1.75; thus, a 57.15% ABV whisky is (57.15%*1.75=100.0125) 100 degrees proof. In the U.S., ABV is converted to alcoholic proof using a ratio of 1:2; thus, a

50% ABV whisky is (50%*2=100) 100-proof whisky.

Pure Malt

See Pure Malt Whisky.

Pure Malt Whisky

Traditionally synonymous to Blended Malt Scotch Whisky, this is a blend of two or more Single Malt Scotch Whiskies from two or more distilleries. Distillers are not allowed to use this designation on their labels.

Purifier

If present on a still, it is attached to the Lyne Arm. The purifier enhances a still's ability to separate/break down alcoholic vapors into fractions.

Quaich

A traditional drinking vessel from Scotland. This cup is quite shallow with a distinctly wide rim and a couple of handles. In the olden days, Scotsmen used it to offer their guests and companions Scotch Whisky (and other spirits).

Reflux

Alcoholic vapors that condense into or revert to liquid spirit while passing through the neck or the Lyne Arm—that is, before reaching the condenser. The reflux returns to the pot for further distillation.

Rummager

A tool usually found in directly fired or directly heated pot stills, this keeps the liquid inside the pot moving at a regular rate, so that whatever solid particles there are will not get deposited to the bottom, where they could easily get burned by the fire underneath the pot.

Rye

A cereal grain that may be used in making beer or whisky.

Saladin Box

Named after its inventor, Charles Saladin, the Saladin Box is a concrete, trough-like container that serves as an alternative to the malting floor and the malting drum. The Saladin Box has a perforated floor; through these small holes, air is blown into the box to aerate the germinating barley. Continuously rotating screw-like mixers, on the other hand, ensure even germination/development.

Sales Maltster

An independent entity that makes malt, and then sells its output to breweries, distilleries, and other businesses/individuals that need them. Sales maltsters also often accept special malt orders, in which case, they make malt according to their clients' specifications.

Scotch

See Scotch Whisky.

Scotch Whisky

Whisky distilled, matured, and bottled in Scotland. To be deserving of the Scotch Whisky name, a whisky must have been made according to and in strict compliance with the guidelines set forth in the Scotch Whisky Regulations of 2009.

Scotch on the Rocks

Scotch Whisky poured over ice.

Scottish Moonshine

See Moonshine.

Shell and Tube Condenser

A type of condenser used in distilleries. It is copper tubing that encases or forms a shell around the Lyne Arm. Water is passed through this tubing, significantly lowering the temperature, and thus inducing the alcoholic vapors to condense into liquid alcohol as they pass through the Lyne Arm.

Single Cask Edition

See Single Cask Scotch Whisky.

Single Cask Scotch Whisky

Scotch Whisky bottled from a single cask; that is, the Scotch Whisky from a single cask is bottled without any top dressing or without first blending it with whisky from a different cask.

Single Grain Scotch Whisky

Scotch Whisky made by a single distillery using water, malted barley, and supplementary grains (e.g., unmalted barley and/or other types of whole grains, malted or unmalted).

Single Malt Scotch

See Single Malt Scotch Whisky.

Single Malt Scotch Whisky

Scotch Whisky made by a single distillery using only water and malted barley; no other cereal may be added to the mix. The term "single" in this designation is a reference to the fact that Single Malt Scotch Whisky must be produced at a single distillery.

Single Single Malt Scotch Whisky

A Single Cask Edition of a Single Malt Scotch Whisky. In other words, it is a Single Malt Scotch Whisky that has been taken from a single cask and has been bottled "untainted" (i.e., without top dressing or without blending with Single Malt Scotch Whiskies from other casks).

Slange Var

"Cheers" in Scottish Gaelic.

Speyside

One of the protected/controlled whisky production regions in Scotland.

Spirit Caramel

The old name of the caramel-colored food coloring, E150a. This term has now been superseded by "plain caramel coloring."

Spirit Safe

This is a box-like contraption that allows the distiller to evaluate the liquid spirit leaving the spirit still. The spirit safe is made of glass, so that the stillman can visually assess the spirit still's distillate. It is also equipped with instruments like hydrometers and thermometers; the stillman uses these instruments to assess which part of the liquid spirit leaving the spirit still is in readily usable form (i.e., the middle cut), and which part of the liquid distillate needs further processing (i.e., the foreshots and feints). However, tasting the spirit in the spirit safe is not allowed, so the spirit safe is sealed shut by the HM Customs and Excise department.

Spirit Still

This is the still that actually produces Scotch Whisky. Low wines are fed into the spirit still, and the resulting distillate (the liquid spirit) is classified into three cuts: the foreshots and the feints, which are returned to the spirit still for further distillation, and the middle cut (the final distillate), which is diverted to a receiving tank for casking.

Spirit Run

The stream of liquid spirit (or the stream of distillate) produced by the spirit still.

Steep

A tank where barley is soaked in water to prepare it for germination during the malting process.

Still

Distillation apparatus. Stills primarily vary by method of distillation (batch or continuous/fractional) and by design (columnar, alembic, Lomond, etc.).

Stillman

The specialist whose main task is to evaluate the liquid spirit leaving the spirit still. He is in charge of separating the distillate into different cuts (i.e., the foreshots, feints, and middle cut) and directing these cuts to their corresponding receivers.

Supplementary Grains

The cereals that are added to malted barley when making Grain Scotch Whisky.

Top Dressing

The process of adjusting the character, depth, and flavor of a whisky, accomplished through the addition of premium or high-quality whisky (usually one of the distillery's oldest or most exceptional single malt whiskies).

Uisge Beatha

The Scottish Gaelic for "water of life."

Unchill-Filtered

See Non-Chill-Filtered

Underback

The container that holds the wort temporarily until the wort has sufficiently cooled down and can be transferred to the washback.

Unfiltered

See Non-Chill-Filtered.

Unmalted Grain

Grain that has not undergone the malting process. Unmalted grains may be added to malted barley and water when making Grain Scotch Whisky.

Usquebaugh

Some say this is an old name for whisky, while others maintain that this old term actually refers to a type of Irish/Scottish liquor that is a mixture of a spirit and spices.

Vatted Malt Whisky

See Pure Malt Whisky.

Vatting

The act of combining two or more whiskies in a single oak cask; this is the start of the "marriage" process.

Volatility

In the context of distillation, this is the tendency of a substance to transition from the liquid phase to the gas phase (in other words—to vaporize).

Warehouse

See Excise Warehouse.

Wash

Produced by fermenting the wort, this is the feedstock used in wash still distillation (the process that produces low wines). This is a beer-like substance with a very low alcohol content (around 8-9% ABV).

Wash Still

The still used in the first distillation. The wash is fed to the wash still to produce the low wines, which will be used in the second distillation (i.e., spirit still distillation).

Washback

A big wooden tub or tank that holds a mixture of wort and yeast. It is where the wort is fermented for a period of several days to create the wash.

Water

One of two major ingredients in the production of Scotch Whisky; the other is malted barley. Distilleries may also use water (as well as plain caramel coloring) as an additive to the final distillate.

Wheat

Whole grains of this cereal may be used (in addition to water and malted barley) to produce Grain Scotch Whisky.

Whiskey

The preferred name for whisky in Ireland and the U.S.

Whisky

A distilled spirit made using water and grain (this can be a single type of grain or a combination of several types of grain).

Whisky Nosing

See Nosing.

Whisky Tasting

The process of evaluating a whisky's character and quality using the senses of sight, smell, taste, and touch.

White Oak

One of the oak species used in making whisky barrels (as well as wine barrels). Scientifically known as the *Quercus alba*, this oak species is native to Eastern North America; thus it is also commonly known as the American oak.

Whole Grains

Cereal grains that have not been refined. A whole grain has all of its parts: the bran, the germ and the endosperm.

Wood Finishes

The woody "flavor" that can be found in Scotch Whisky. This can be attributed to the maturation period that the whisky undergoes in oak casks. After the initial oak aging, moreover, distilleries may transfer their whisky to a different oak cask and age it further for a period of several months to enhance the whisky's wood finish.

Worm Tub

An old type of condenser. The worm tub consists of a spiral tube (made of copper) through which alcoholic vapors pass after leaving the Lyne Arm. This spiral tube is immersed in a tub of cold water; traditionally, the tub is located outside where it can collect rainwater. The water in the tub cools the spiral tube; thus the alcoholic vapors within the tube condense into liquid spirit.

Wort

The sugar-rich liquid produced after prolonged and continuous stirring of the mash (grist plus hot water) in the mash tun. The wort is transferred to the underback, where it is cooled, and then subsequently transferred to the washback for fermentation.

Year

In the context of whisky production, this can refer to the bottling year or the distillation year.

Yeast

An essential ingredient in fermentation. Yeast is added to the wort to produce the wash, which is the raw material used in the first distillation (wash still distillation).

General Index

alchemists, 31. *See also* distillation

alcohol by volume, 51, 196, 211. *See also* alcoholic strength; proof

alcoholic strength by volume, 4. *See* alcohol by volume

alcoholic strength, 52, 62, 64, 69, 70, 73. *See also* alcohol by volume; proof

alembic still. *See* still, types of: pot

Amendment to the United States Constitution: Eighteenth, 115-116; Twenty-first, 116

American white oak. *See* white oak

anCnoc, 152

angel's share, 196

aqua vitae, 10, 23-24. *See also* uisge beatha

aromas, 196; assessing, 68, 71, 73, 74; definition of, 65-66; effect of ice on, 79-80; influence of geography on, 64-65; Scotch Whisky Research Institute's Flavour Wheel, **67**; whisky aromas kit, 75-76. *See also* tasting through the sense of smell: flavors; Single Malt Whisky Flavour Map, The

arrack, 111, 111n

astringent, 70. *See also* tasting through the sense of touch: mouth-feel

B

barley grains, 33, 42-43. *See* malted barley

barrel, 41, 197. *See also* oak cask: types

bartenders, 113, 114, 115, 117-118

beer (fermentation output). *See* wash

beer, mum, 20

Beveridge, Jim, 93; Single Malt Whisky Flavour Map, The, 93, **94**, 95-96. *See also* single malt Scotch cluster classification system

blend, 197

blended grain Scotch. *See under* Scotch whisky categories

blended malt Scotch. *See under* Scotch whisky categories

blended malt whisky, 198. *See* Scotch whisky categories: blended malt

blended Scotch. *See under* Scotch whisky categories

blending, 55, 104, 198

Bordeaux, 41, 199

bottling process, **42**

bottling year, 105, 197

Bourbon, 41, 61, 62, 199, 201

box malting. 45. *See* Saladin box. *See also* malting: germination stage

brewer maltster. *See under* maltster

brightness. *See* tasting through the sense of sight: clarity

Broom, Dave, 93. Single Malt Whisky Flavour Map, The, 93, **94**, 95-96. *See also* single malt Scotch cluster classification system

butt, 41, 198. *See also* oak cask: types

C

Calvados, 41, 199

Campbeltown, 102, **161**, 198; active single malt Scotch distilleries, 161-163; closed single malt Scotch distilleries; 184-189; single malts, characteristics of, 102. *See also* protected whisky localities

caramel coloring. *See* plain caramel coloring

cask strength (alcoholic strength), 56, 69, 199. *See also* alcoholic strength

casking process, **42**, 53-54

cereal, 197, 199, 207, 212, 215, 217

charring, 199-200

chill filtering, 56-57, 62, 63, 200

chill filtration. *See* chill filtering

chill haze, 56, 57, 63. *See* clouding

chill-filtered, 63, 64, 1 05

clarity. *See under* tasting through the sense of sight

clouding, 35, 56, 72

coal. *See under* fuel

coastal. 105, 200; distilleries, 105; warehouse, 55

cocktail, 112-117

Coffey still. *See* still, types of: column

Cognac, 41, 199

color. *See under* tasting through the sense of sight

columnar still. *See* still, types of: column

condenser, 40, 201; shell and tube, 213; worm tub, 217-218

congeners, 201

continuous distillation. *See* distillation: fractional

continuous still. *See* still, types of: column

cooling mechanism. *See* condenser

cooling stones, 84-85

cooper, 199, 201

copper, 38, 39, 40, 213, 217

Cor, John (friar), 10, 23

corn, 201

Council Directive: 80/777/EEC, 34 (see natural mineral waters directive); 98/83/EC, 34 (see drinking water directive)

creamy, 70. *See also* tasting through the sense of touch: mouth-feel

culm, 47. *See also* process waste

Currie, Andrew, 136n

cut, 201. *See also* distillate fractions; feints; foreshot; heart of the run

D

deactivated distilleries, 123; list of, 189

deculming, 47

depth filter sheet, 56, 63

dilution, 56, 68, 72, 74-75. *See also* etiquette: on adding water

direct firing. *See* direct heating

direct heating, 39

distillate fractions, 51, 52-53

distillate, 29, 51, 52, 196, 202

distillation, 29-30, 202; batch, 197, 206, 211; fractional, 200, 204; history of, 30-32; pot still, 7, 34, 37; of Scotch whisky, ban, 12, 17; of Scotch whisky, illegal, 14; in Scotland, history of, 32; of single malt Scotch, equipment, 7, 37-41; of single malt Scotch, ingredients, 32-37; spirit still, **42**, 52; wash still, **42**, 50, 51; year, 105

distiller maltster. *See under* maltster

distillery, 202

double cask. *See under* single malt Scotch types

double casking, 104

double distilled. *See under* single malt Scotch types

draff, 49, 202. *See also* process waste

dram, 202

drinking water directive, 34

drum malting. 45, 202. *See also* malting: germination stage

Dumbuck (the single malt brand), 178. *See also* Littlemill (Index of Closed and Deactivated Distilleries)

Dunglass (the single malt brand), 178. *See also* Littlemill (Index of Closed and Deactivated Distilleries)

E

E150a, 37, 211. *See* plain caramel coloring

Edinburgh Guild of Barber Surgeons, The, 11, 23, 24

endogenous enzyme systems, 3, 203, 204

etiquette, 76-77; on adding ice, 78-80; on adding water, 81-82; on cooling stones, 84-85; on drinking it long, 80-81; on drinking it neat, 82; on glassware, 82-84; on mixing, 80-81

European oak, 41, 61

Exchequer Rolls 1494, 10, 23

excise on malt, 12, 14, 19, 20-21. *See also under* Acts of the Scottish Parliament

excise on Scotch whisky. *See under* Acts of the Scottish Parliament

excise warehouse, 54, 203

exciseman. *See* gauger

F

feedstock, 203

feints receiver, 52, 201

feints, 52, 203

fermentation, 3, **42**, 50, 203-204

filtering, 56. *See also* chill filtering

filtration. *See* filtering

finish. *See under* tasting through the sense of smell

finishing, 55

first cut. *See* foreshot

first fraction. *See* foreshot

fizzy, 70. *See also* tasting through the sense of touch: mouth-feel

flavor descriptors, 71. *See* tasting through the sense of smell: flavors

flavor map. *See* Single Malt Whisky Flavour Map, The

flavor wheel. *See* Scotch Whisky Research Institute's Flavour Wheel

flavors. *See under* tasting through the sense of smell

floor malting, 45, 204. *See also* malting: germination stage foreshot, 52, 204

foreshot receiver, 52

fuel: coal, 39; natural gas, 39, 46, 47; peat, 46, 47, 211

G

gauger, 204

geographical factors, 64-65

germination, 43-45, 204

glassware. *See* whisky glass: types. *See also under* etiquette

Glen Deveron (the single malt brand), 153. *See also* MacDuff (Index of Active Single Malt Scotch Distilleries)

Glen Flagler (the single malt brand), 177. *See also* Moffat (Index of Closed and Deactivated Distilleries)

Glen Scotia (the single malt brand), 102. *See also* Glen Scotia (Index of Active Distilleries)

Glencairn glass, 84. *See also* whisky glass: types

grain distillery, 204

grain Scotch. *See under* Scotch whisky types

green malt, 44, 45, 46

grist, 34, 48, 49, 205

grist hopper, 48

guaranteed age whisky, 205. *See also* age statement

H

hard water, 35, 72

Hazelburn (the single malt brand), 102, 162. *See also* Springbank (Index of Active Distilleries)

heads. *See* foreshot

heart of the run, 52-53

Highland, 97-98, **126**, 127, 163, 205. *See also* protected whisky regions

Highland line, 97

Highland Park (the single malt brand), 103. *See also* Highland Park (Index of Active Distilleries)

Highland, active single malt Scotch distilleries: East Highlands, 127-128; North Highlands, 128-131; South Highlands, 131-133; West Highlands, 133-134

Highland, closed single malt Scotch distilleries: East Highlands, 163-166; North Highlands, 166-169; South Highlands, 169-171; West Highlands, 171 hogshead, 41, 205. *See also* oak cask: types

How to Mix Drinks, or the Bon-Vivant's Companion, 111-112, 115. *See also under* Thomas, Jerry

hydrometer, 205

I

inner pipe coil, 40. *See also* worm

intermediate still, 106. *See also* single malt Scotch types: triple distilled; spirit still; wash still

internal heating coil, 39

internal heating cylinder, 39-40

Inverness records, 23-24

Islands, 103-104, **135**, 172, 205; active single malt Scotch distilleries, 135-138; closed single malt Scotch distilleries, 172; single malts, characteristics of, 103-104. *See also* protected whisky regions

Islay, 101-102, **157**, 182, 205; active single malt Scotch distilleries, 157-160; closed single malt Scotch distilleries, 182-184; single malts, characteristics of, 101-102. *See also* protected whisky localities

Isle of Islay. *See* Islay

Islebrae (the single malt brand), 178. *See also* Moffat (Index of Closed and Deactivated Distilleries)

J

James IV (king of Scotland), 23

James VI (king of Scotland), 24

K

Kilkerran (the single malt brand), 102, 162-163. *See also* Glengyle (Index of Active Distilleries)

Killyloch (the single malt brand), 178. *See also* Moffat (Index of Closed and Deactivated Distilleries)

kilning process, 45-47

L

Lafranconi, Francesco, 118; Lafranconi Scotch Cocktails, 118-120

LaPointe, François-Joseph, 90. *See also* single malt Scotch cluster classification system

Le Nez du Vin, 75

Ledaig (the single malt brand), 103-104, 138n. *See also* Tobermory (Index of Active Distilleries)

marriage, 208, 216. *See* marrying

marrying, 55

mash tun, **48**, 49, 208

mash, 48, 49, 208

mashing machine, 48

mashing, **42**, 48, 208

master blender, 209

maturation. *See* oak maturation

middle cut, 209. *See* heart of the run

milling, 48

mineral water, 72. *See also* natural mineral waters directive

mixologist, 81, 118

mixology, 109, 117; father of (*see* Thomas, Jerry); history of 110-117

monasteries, dissolution. *See* Acts of the Scottish Parliament: Annexation of the Temporalities of Benefices to the Crown

monks, displacement, 11, 18

moonshine, 14, 209. *See* Scottish moonshine phase

Mosstowie (the single malt brand), 154. *See also* Miltonduff (Index of Active Distilleries)

mothballed distilleries. *See* deactivated distilleries

mothballing, 189

mouth-coating, 70. *See also* tasting through the sense of touch: mouth-feel

mouth-warming, 70. *See also* tasting through the sense of touch: mouth-feel

N

nasal effects. *See* tasting through the sense of touch: nose-feel

natural gas. *See under* fuel

natural mineral waters directive, 34

NEAT™ (Naturally Engineered Aroma Technology) glass, 84. *See also* whisky glass: types

neck, 38, 209-210. *See also* still, types of: pot

new-make, 60. *See* raw spirit

non-malted barley, 14-15

nose-drying, 70. *See also* tasting through the sense of touch: nose-feel

nose-warming, 70. *See also* tasting through the sense of touch: nose-feel nosing glass, 208. *See* snifter, tulip-shaped

nosing, 210. *See also* tasting through the sense of smell; tasting through the sense of touch

O

oak cask, 53-55 passim, 196, 198; effect on color, 60-62; most popular, 199; refilling, 41 (*see also* charring); second-hand, 41, 55, 61, 196, 197; types, 40-41, 198-199

oak maturation, 54-55, 209

octave, 41. *See also* oak cask: types

odors. *See* aromas; tasting through the sense of smell: flavors

olfactory memory. *See* scent memory. *See also* Le Nez du Vin

olfactory receptors, 66, 68, 76

organic whisky, 210

organoleptic properties, 59, 79

organoletic profile, 60

orthonasal olfaction, 66. *See also* tasting through the sense of smell

P

paddle, 211. *See also* germination

pagoda, 211. *See also* malt kiln

Papal authority, renunciation of. *See* Acts of the Scottish Parliament: Papal Jurisdiction Act 1560

patent still. *See* still, types of: column

peat. *See* under fuel

plain caramel coloring, 32, 37, 211

Port, 41, 61, 62, 199

pot ale, 51. *See also* process waste

prickle, 70. *See also* tasting through the sense of touch: nose-feel

process waste: culm, 47; draff, 49, 202; pot ale, 51; lees, 52

prohibition, 115-116

proof, 211-212. *See also* alcohol by volume

protected whisky localities, 101-102

protected whisky regions, 96-101

punch, 110-112

pungent, 69. *See also* tasting through the sense of touch: nose-feel

pure malt whisky, 198, 212. *See* Scotch whisky categories: blended malt

purifier, 212

Q

quaich, 212

quarter, 41. *See also* oak cask: types

Quercus alba, 41, 217. *See* white oak

R

raw spirit, 38, 53-54

raw whisky. *See* raw spirit

reflux bowl, 38

reflux, 212

retronasal olfaction, 66. *See also* tasting through the sense of smell

rummager, 39, 212

rye, 212

S

Saccharomyces cerevisiae, 37. *See* yeast

safe. *See* spirit safe

Saladin box, 45, 212-213. *See also* malting: germination stage

sales maltster. *See under* maltster

scent memory, 66, 68, 76. *See also* Le Nez du Vin

scents. *See* aromas; tasting through the sense of smell: flavors

scorching, 39, 40

Scotch whisky categories: blended, 6, 81, 198; blended grain, 6, 197 (*see also* Scotch whisky types: grain), blended malt, 6, 198, 212 (*see also* Scotch whisky types: malt); single grain, 6, 205, 213 (*see also* Scotch whisky types: grain); single malt, 6-7, 214 (*see also* Scotch whisky types: malt)

Scotch Whisky Regulations of 2009, 3, 15, 213; on additional substances, 211; on aging, 41, 54, 209; on alcohol by volume, 196; on aroma, 196; on the pot still, 37; on warehousing, 203; on water, 34; on whisky regions, 96, 97, 103

Scotch Whisky Research Institute's Flavour Wheel, **67**. *See also* aromas

Scotch whisky types: cask strength, 199, grain, 15, 205; grain, origin, 14-15; malt, 15, 207; single cask, 213. *See also* single malt Scotch types

Scotch whisky, 2-3, 213; characteristics of, 3-5; cocktails (*see under* Lafranconi, Francesco); exportation, 5, 16-17; history, 10-15; importation ban, 18, 20; on the rocks, 78, 85, 213 (*see also* etiquette: on adding ice); taxes, 12-15 passim (*see also* Acts of the Scottish Parliament); unofficial region (*see* Islands)

Springbank (the single malt brand), 102, 162. *See also* Springbank (Index of Active Distilleries)

steep, 215

steeping. *See under* malting

still, 37, 211, 215

still, types of: column, 200-201; Lomond, 206; pot, 7, 37-40, 211

stillman, 51-52, 53, 215

supplementary grains, 215

T

tails. *See* feints

Talisker (the single malt brand), 103. *See also* Talisker (Index of Active Distilleries)

tannins, 41. *See also* charring

Tapputi-Belatekallim, 31

taste descriptors, 71

taste receptors, 71

tasting glass, 72. *See also* whisky glass: types

tasting through the sense of sight: clarity, 60, 62-64, 72; color: 60-62; viscosity, 62

tasting through the sense of smell: aromas (*see* aromas); flavors, 66, **67**, 68, 74, 79; aftertaste, 69, 74; finish, 69. *See also* Single Malt Whisky Flavour Map, The

tasting through the sense of taste, 70-71, 74

tasting through the sense of touch: mouth-feel, 70, 209; nose-feel, 69-70, 73, 210

tasting: preparation, 71-72; step by step guide, 72-75

tears. *See* legs

texture, 70. *See* tasting through the sense of touch: mouth-feel

third cut. *See* feints

third fraction. *See* feints

Thomas, Jerry (Jeremiah P. Thomas), 111-112, 114-115; How to Mix Drinks, or the Bon-Vivant's Companion, 111-112, 115

Tobermory (the single malt brand), 103-104. *See also* Tobermory (Index of Active Distilleries)

top dressing, 215. *See also* marrying

triple distilled. *See under* single malt Scotch types

U

uisge beatha, 2, 9-10, 215. *See also* aqua vitae

unchill-filtered. *See* single malt Scotch types: non-chill-filtered

underback, 49, 215

unfiltered. *See* single malt Scotch types: non-chill-filtered

unmalted barley. *See* non-malted barley

unmalted grain, 216. *See also* non-malted barley

unofficial whisky region. *See* Islands

used cask, 41. *See* oak cask: second-hand

usquebaugh, 216

V

vatted malt whisky. *See* Scotch whisky categories: blended malt

vatting, 216

vermouth, 115

vintage single malt Scotch. *See under* single malt Scotch types

vintage year statement, 105

viscosity. *See under* tasting through the sense of sight

volatility, 29, 202, 216

W

warehouse: location, 55; vat, 53

wash, 37, 38, 50-51, 204, 216. *See also* feedstock

wash charger: 50, 51

wash still, 38, 51, 216; distillation (*see under* distillation)

washback, 49, 50, 216

water, 216; legal requirements, 34; for tasting, 72; types, 34-36; uses in distillation, 34, 39, 40, 43, 48, 55

water steeping. *See* malting: steeping stage

whiskey, 1-2, 217

whisky, 1-2, 217; openness, 68, 74; regions (*see* single malt Scotch classification: by region)

whisky aromas kit, 75-76. *See also* Le Nez du Vin; scent memory

whisky glass, 71-72; types, 83-84

whisky glass, thistle-shaped, 83. *See also* whisky glass: types whisky tot glass, Bottega del Vino, **62**, 84. *See also* whisky glass: types

whisky tumbler: traditional, 83; elongated, 83. *See also* whisky glass: types

white oak, 41, 61, 217. *See also* oak cask

whole grains, 217. *See also* cereal

Wishart, David, 88. *See also* single malt Scotch cluster classification system

worm, 40. *See also* condenser

worm tub. *See under* condenser

wort, 49, 204, 208, 218

Y

yeast, 4, 32, 36-37, 50, 203-204, 218

Index of
Single Malt
Scotch Distilleries

Index of **ACTIVE** Distilleries

Dailuaine, 146
Dalmore, 129
Dalwhinnie, 133
Deanston, 132
Dufftown, 146

E

Edradour, 132

F

Fettercairn, Old, 127

G

Glen Elgin, 147
Glen Garioch, 127-128
Glen Grant, 147
Glen Moray, 147
Glen Ord, 130
Glen Scotia, 53, 102, 162
Glen Spey, 147
Glenallachie, 147-148
Glenburgie, 148
Glencadam, 127
GlenDronach, 148
Glendullan , 148-149
Glenfarclas, 149
Glenfiddich, 149
Glenglassaugh, 149-150
Glengoyne, 134
Glengyle, 102, 162-163
Glenkinchie, 141
Glenlivet, 150
Glenlossie, 150

Glenmorangie, 129-130
Glenrothes, 150
Glentauchers, 150-151
Glenturret, 132

H

Highland Park, 103, 135, 137. *See also* Highland Park (the single malt brand) in the General Index

I

Inchgower, 151
Isle of Arran, 104, 136
Isle of Barra, 104, 136
Isle of Jura, 104, 137

K

Kilchoman, 102, 159-160
Kininvie, 151
Knockando, 151-152
Knockdhu, 152

L

Lagavulin, 101, 160
Laphroaig, 101, 102, 160
Linkwood, 152
Loch Lomond, 127, 134
Lochnagar, 128
Longmorn, 152

M

Macallan, 152-153

MacDuff , 153
Mannochmore, 153
Milltown. *See* Strathisla
Miltonduff, 153-154
Mortlach, 154

O

Oban, 134

P

Pulteney, Old, 130

R

Roseisle, 154
Royal Brackla, 130

S

Scapa, 103, 137-138
Speyburn, 154-155
Speyside, 155
Springbank, 102, 162
Strathisla, 155
Strathmill, 155-156

T

Talisker, 103, 138
Tamdhu, 156
Tamnavulin, 156
Teaninich, 131
Tobermory, 103, 138. *See also* To-

bermory (the single malt brand) in
the General Index
Tomatin, 131
Tomintoul, 156
Tormore, 156
Tullibardine, 132-133

Index of **CLOSED** and **DEACTIVATED** Distilleries

A

Abbeyhill, 172
Albyn, 184
Ardenistiel, 182
Ardlussa, 184
Ardmore, 182
Argyll on Longrow, 185
Argyll on Lorne St., 185
Auchinblae, 163
Auchnagie, 169
Auchorachan, 180
Auchtermuchty, 172
Auchtertool, 172
Avonglen, 172

B

Ballechin, 169
Ballegreggan, 185
Banff, 166
Bank, 172
Ben Morven, 166-167

McKinnon's Distillery. *See* Argylle on Lorne St.

Meadowburn, 188

Millburn, 169

Millfield, 166

Milltown, 169

Moffat, 178

Montrose. *See* Glenesk

Mossfield, 188

Mountain Dew, 188

Mulchaich, 168

Mulendry. *See* Mulindry

Mulindry, 183

N

Nevis, 171

Newington. *See* Edinburgh

Newton, 184

North Esk. *See* Glenesk

North Port, 166

O

Octomore, 184

Old Rome, 179

P

Parkmore, 181

Pittyvaich, 181-182

Port Charlotte. *See* Lochindaal

Port Ellen, 184

R

Rhinns. *See* Lochindaal

Rieclachan, 188

Rosebank, 179

Ryefield, 168

S

Seggie, 179

Springside, 188

Stornoway, 172

Strathdee, 166

Stratheden. *See* Auchtermuchty

Strathmore, 179

Stronachie, 170

Sunbury, 179

T

Tallant, 184

Tambowie, 180

Toberanrigh, 188

Tochineal, 182

Tomdachoill, 170

Towiemore, 182

U

Union, 188

Upper Cragabus, 184

W

West Highland, 189

West Sciennes. *See* Edinburgh

Westerkepp, 170-171. *See also* Kepp

Y

Yardheads, 180

Index of
Water Sources